3557
$27.95

D1526560

IDENTITY AND INTIMACY IN TWINS

Identity and Intimacy in TWINS

BARBARA SCHAVE AND JANET CIRIELLO

PRAEGER

PRAEGER SPECIAL STUDIES • PRAEGER SCIENTIFIC

Library of Congress Cataloging in Publication Data

Schave, Barbara.
    Identity and intimacy in twins.

    Bibliography: p.
    Includes index.
    1. Twins—Psychology. 2. Identity (Psychology)
3. Intimacy (Psychology) I. Ciriello, Janet. II. Title.
[DNLM: 1. Twins—Psychology. 2. Identification
(Psychology) 3. Object attachment. 4. Sibling
relations. WS 105.5.F2 S313i]
BF723.T9S28 1983   155.4'44   83–13828
ISBN 0–03–068924–4

For keeping us aware of the needs of others, including the needs of twins, we dedicate this book to Carlo, Douglas, Elizabeth, Matthew, Nicholas, Nick, Richard, and Roman.

Published in 1983 by Praeger Publishers
CBS Educational and Professional Publishing
a Divison of CBS Inc.
521 Fifth Avenue, New York, NY 10175, U.S.A

© 1983 by Praeger Publishers

56789 052 9876543

Printed in the United States of America
on acid-free paper.

ACKNOWLEDGMENTS

Writing this book provided us with an opportunity to meet a group of generous and fascinating twins. We are grateful that they chose to share so much about twinships with us because, obviously, we could not have written this book without them. They also encouraged greater reflection about ourselves and our experiences as twins.

We feel particularly grateful to Douglas Schave, M.D. for the many thoughtful questions and comments about our work and for the many hours he spent at the word processor.

We thank Nick Ciriello for managing our efforts until our editor George Zimmar guided us to this final product. George combined good humor with an understanding of the child development issues that we raise in this book. And he knew what had to be done!

We also wish to acknowledge Tonya Gruenewald for so pleasantly handling certain typing and reproduction tasks.

PREFACE

Our interest in writing this book was both personal and professional. We are both members of different identical twin pairs. Our knowledge of child development, clinical psychology, and of the knowledge to date on twin development led us to conclude that there are large gaps in the accrued knowledge about twinship. We believed that mental health professionals, developmental psychologists, clinical psychologists, child development researchers, parents of twins and twins themselves would profit from a broader understanding of twinship.

Specifically, we wanted to know what it was like for other twins to grow up as twins. Our attempt was also to dispel some of the mythology that has grown up around twinship. Twins have been portrayed in mythology and in world literature in many symbolic ways. They have been seen as opposites of one another, copies of each other, halves of a whole, and at times even as freaks. Popular literature and the media have relied heavily on sinister images of twins and have frequently emphasized the mysterious and dramatic fantasies that people foster about twinship.

We wanted to go beyond these images of duality and enrich the meaning of twinship. Interviews with 20 sets of adult identical twins and 20 sets of adult fraternal twins provided us with material which added to our understanding of twinship and hopefully to the reader's understanding of a unique circumstance of development.

This book is organized so that the reader first comes to understand what research is available to date on twinship. Secondly, an overview of identity formation in twins and single children is presented. The remainder of the book describes the interviews we conducted which focused on identity and intimacy in twinship as reported by the 40 sets of adult twins who participated in this study.

Barbara Schave, Ed.D.
Janet Ciriello, Ed.D.
Los Angeles, Ca.

CONTENTS

1

AN OVERVIEW OF TWINS IN
PSYCHOLOGICAL RESEARCH

Twins have been considered a source of wonder and fascination, repulsion, and fear since the beginning of recorded history. Mythology presents twins with special powers of good and evil. In legends, folktales, and primitive religions, twins have been attributed with heroic and magical powers. It was not until Darwin postulated his theory of evolution that twin studies were used by researchers to determine the importance of genetics in human development.

Since the first studies of twins in the late nineteenth century to the present time, there has been a proliferation of research. Early studies focused primarily on the nature-nurture controversy. Twin interaction and the twinning bond were then recognized by researchers. In-depth case studies by psychoanalysts presented personality development either from a healthy or from an abnormal point of view (Hift 1980). Language development studies have indicated that within the twin pair the twin with the more developed language acquisition is the more dominant (Koch 1966). Studies on parental attitudes toward twins indicate that parental treatment is crucial in determining individuality in twins (Lytton 1980; Paluszny and Gibson 1974). In the controversial issue of heritability of intelligence, twins have been used to prove the superiority of the white race (Brody and Brody 1976). Most recently, Bouchard's popularly fascinating studies of identical twins reared apart tantalize us with histories of twins suggesting the dominant role of genetic blueprinting in an explanation of similarities between these subjects (Holden 1980). This study returns to the initial interest in twin development—the nature-nurture controversy.

Twin development has been viewed from many perspectives. There is a lack of consensus among researchers as to what contributions twin studies make to an understanding of human development and, more specifically, of twin development. In this chapter we will attempt to build bridges between the large and diversified body of information available and the theories that exist concerning twins. Particular interest will be placed on the unique psychological development of twins.

Sir Francis Galton (Mittler 1971), a mathematician of the late nineteenth century, was the first to suggest that twins could be used as subjects for studies that investigated the relative contribution of heredity as compared with environment. His assumption was that physically similar twins were the products of identical genetic structures. Galton was, then, the founder of a scientific method using twin subjects.

Not until the late 1930s were actual case studies conducted of identical twins reared apart. These classic case studies of identical twins reared apart (e.g., see Newman, Freeman, and Holzinger 1937) were the bases for over 121 studies that have been conducted by researchers in the last 45 years (Juels-Nielsen 1965; Shields 1962). The predominant interests of these researchers were the physical similarities between twins, their measurable personality traits, and their intelligence. Such case studies were used primarily to demonstrate the genetic components of intelligence. Although personality development was considered in these studies, the lack of an agreed-upon theoretical definition of *personality* made comparison among these studies impossible.

Twins, both identical and fraternal, reared apart or together, then became the "ideal" subjects for psychological researchers, as so many arguments, pro and con, nature or nurture, could be fueled with such data.

INTELLIGENCE AND COGNITION The most definitive and consistent research findings on twins indicate that intelligence, as measured by standardized intelligence tests, is genetically determined. Comparisons of identical and fraternal twins show identical twins to be more similar than fraternal twins on intelligence measures. Although different standardized tests have been used as measurement instruments, the correlation between identical twins on intelligence is approximated to be between 0.79 and 0.88 when reared together, and 0.925 and 0.99 when reared apart. The correlation for fraternal twins is approximated to be between 0.5 and 0.6 (Jensen 1969; Koch 1966; Mittler 1971; Newman et al. 1937; Shields 1962). The notably lower correlation in intelligence of identical twins reared together as compared with those reared apart, is provocative. Could it be, that identical twins reared together develop more differently from each other than those reared apart? Do the differences encouraged and supported in the backgrounds of such twins, lead to variations in tested intellectual abilities? Why, indeed, do identical twins reared apart have more similar tested intelligence? No statistical data have come to light about the correlation on intelligence between fraternal twins reared apart. The only contradiction to these findings is reported by Farber (1981), who in a statistically sophisticated study finds a 0.7 correlation on intelligence scores for identical twins reared apart. Research, using small samples or case studies, indicates that intelligence remains stable throughout the lives of twins (Burlingham 1952; Gessell 1941; Osborne and Suddick 1973).

Cognitive psychologists have found that identical twins are more similar than fraternal twins on measures of cognitive development. Indications from these studies are that identical twins, whether reared apart or together, have parallel development throughout the stages of cognitive development, as described by Piaget (1932), displaying a high concordance for the spurts and lags between stages as well as for the final cognitive level attained (Farber 1981; Wilson 1975). These studies of cognitive development not only clarify the importance of the genetic blueprint, but they also suggest that cognition is more strongly influenced by genetics than by noncognitive variables, which appear to be more affected by parental ties and the environment (Matheny, Dolan, and Wilson 1976).

LANGUAGE   Language acquisition in twins has
ACQUISITION   been an area of particular interest to
psychologists. Early studies substantiated observations that
young twins often have inferior language development as
compared with single children (Davis 1937). Throughout the
1960s and 1970s many researchers looked at aspects of
language development in twins. The results of these studies are
diverse, as they deal with different aspects of language
acquisition.

Koch (1966) hypothesized that twins have unique difficulties in learning to speak because of general mental retardation
due to prenatal abnormalities and economically deprived home
environments. However, other researchers (Munsinger and
Douglas 1976; Wilson and Harring 1977) emphasize that
language impoverishment in twins is related to genetic
components, playing down the home impoverishment factors.

Another point of view is also prevalent in the literature.
Several authors (Black and Campbell 1974; Burlingham 1952;
Koch 1966; Mittler 1971) have indicated that twins—in particular, identical twins—have less incentive to learn to speak
because they understand each other adequately through
nonverbal communication. These studies stress that because of
the dependence of twins on each other and the treatment they
frequently receive as a unit instead of as individuals they have
limited individual experiences with adults and other children.
They do not develop sufficient language experiences in
relation to the self to develop the necessary egocentric speech
patterns. Furthermore, twins are poor speech models for each
other, and they often develop their own language, which
complicates and may even retard language acquisition.

Language theorists Luria and Yudovitch (1959) speculate
that language retardation can be attributed to the "twin
situation" in which neither twin is faced with a real necessity
to communicate with other children or adults, since the
communication between the twins is easier and more
satisfying. Luria predicted and showed that separating twins
would accelerate language development because each twin
would be forced to communicate with others in his/her own
environment. This forced separation was followed by intensive

special training given to the less well developed speaker of the twin pair. It is difficult to discern whether the improvement in language was due to training or to separation. It is extremely questionable whether the less developed twin would have thrived without special training. Luria's method of separating twins to improve language development is not a method that most parents of twins would use to accelerate language acquisition.

The psychoanalytic point of view, as expressed by Burlingham (1952) and Leonard (1961), indicates that problems with language acquistion in twins are more complicated. Their research and observations suggest that because of the extremely close nature of the twin bond, twins identify with each other, which results in only partial differentiation of their ego structures. Because of these difficulties in their individual abilities to form separate and unique identities, unit identity emerges. This unit identity confuses communication with the outside world. Unit identity allows intertwin communication to be nonverbal or indiscernible to their parents or primary caretakers. This situation is intensified when twins are treated as a unit and when they are permitted to remain in each other's company almost exclusively. Initially, this constant companionship is easier for the family, but later it creates problems in language development as well as problems with the process of individuation and separation between the pair members.

Lytton (1980), a psychologist, concluded from his enthnographic research that the twin situation affects the socialization practices of parents and is more influential than social class differences in shaping parent-child interaction. Lytton also contends that the most important determinant of the unique pattern of language acquisition that twins exhibit is fewer verbal interactions of all kinds. In his research, twins received fewer demonstrations of affection than single children, even after allowing for differences in the mother's education. The conclusion of the study was that the parents' reduced verbal interaction with their twins reduced the twins' speech attempts. The findings clearly state that there is reciprocity in the parent-child interaction. The parent is a stronger determinant of speech development than the child. It can be concluded from this study that parents play a major role in the adequate or inadequate speech development of their twin children.

The most recent research by Malstrom (1980), following Koch's line of reasoning, was an observational study of her own twins' language development from the ages of 3-4 years. She concluded that the children's twin status was reflected in their syntax and lexicon by their use of double names for themselves and others and by their use of *me* to refer to themselves together. She suggests that the strong bond among experience, language, and cognition makes twin language a manifestation of the twinship. More research on twin language will indicate whether Malstrom's (1980) reported "manifestations of the twin bond" is a developmental stage in twin language. Interestingly, Malstrom also suggests that these manifestations of the twin bond might be a useful index to the relative strength of the pair's twin identity and identity as individuals.

In looking at the studies reported in the preceding pages, it is apparent that the findings of these various research projects are contradictory. While some studies clearly focused on twins, other studies used twin subjects in an attempt to explain some area of child development. The research on intelligence and cognition favors genetic components as the most significant of developmental determinants. The language acquisition research adds social factors including environment, parental influence, and the intertwin relationship and leads to broader developmental conclusions about twins.

PERSONALITY DEVELOPMENT   Personality research concerning twins becomes even more complicated for several reasons. Among these is an earlier-noted disagreement concerning the definition of *personality*. In addition psychologists have employed twin subjects for their particular interest in the components of a personality variable (e.g., introversion-extroversion) with no interest in twin personality development. Psychoanalytic orientation has been both clinical and developmental, but the thrust of the material is based on case studies of "troubled" twin subjects. Therefore, this literature deals generally with problems of personality development. It is important to keep these limitations in mind when reviewing the research on personality development in twins.

Early case studies of twins suggested a genetic component to temperament, activity level, and social ability (Newman et al. 1937). More recent studies (Goldsmith and Gottesman 1981; Matheny 1980; Matheny et al. 1976; Plomin and Willerman 1975; Torgensen and Kringlen 1978) confirm this early research by indicating that at least half of these personality traits of temperament, reflectivity-impulsivity, and social ability are determined by genetic endowments. For example, an amazingly large study of 12,898 Swedish twin pairs (Floderus-Myrhed, Pederson, and Rasmuson 1980) using the short form of Eysenck's Introversion/Extroversion Scale demonstrated that at least 50% of this personality trait is genetically determined.

Although the research on differences in personality development in twins is less well based scientifically, there is a certain appreciation for the totality of twin experiences that is absent in the research that concentrates on singular personality traits. The majority of research on twins reared together demonstrates that more differences are found in personality because of the significance of the environment on its determination (Farber 1981; Lytton 1980). This research looks at behavioral differences in twin development. Consensus among researchers is clear on one point: Differences in twin personality, as measured by parameters of behavior, are present at birth. Gifford, Muraski, Brazelton, and Young (1966)—in their case study of identical twins born to educated middle-class parents, from birth to age 4—conclude:

> In identical twins, accidental differences in size, behavior and rate of maturation are present at birth, presumably the result of differences in the intrauterine environment. These physical and behavioral differences established the original basis for

certain individual characteristics in the developing ego of each twin.
Although these differences are not genetically determined they have
some enduring qualities of constitutional predisposition. (p.266)

These researchers observed differences in twins from
birth in sensorimotor maturation and selective use of intelligence, which continued as individual, autonomous ego
tendencies in the differentiation of each twin. These ego
tendencies undergo complex interactions with parental
attitudes and the relationship between the twins. During
relatively healthy development, the parents' "differential
identifications" with their twins follow their individual
characteristics and alter appropriately when the twins'
behavior changes. The Gifford et al. study contends that the
unfolding of the personality is a combination of the meshing
of factors, the innate with the experiential or environmental
factors. This study indicates that normally developing twins
will show behavioral differences. In other words, this study
clarifies what many parents may have suspected: that
differential treatment of children, even of twins, and differing
relationships with the environment (including parents) result
in children who have their own personality characteristics.
This result comes about in spite of the fact that so much has
been determined by biological and constitutional factors.

Burlingham (1952, 1963), who has written extensively on
twin development, conducted three case studies of institution-
alized identical twins. Her observations at the Hampstead
Clinic in London, and in the follow-up meetings later in the
twins' lives, showed that the twins studied had many characteristics in common. However, there were differences in
personality significant enough to differentiate their
development, their emotional problems, and their life choices.
As infants one twin was more sensitive and responsive, and
the other twin was more indifferent or cold. Burlingham
states that these differences were not a result of birth order.
However, Werner's (1973) study indicates the birth sequence
is the determining factor in behavioral differences in a
multiracial group of twins.

Smith (1976), observing his own identical twins, records
that from birth to the age of 9, the boys showed nearly identical

development of biological characteristics but markedly differing personalities. From the time of birth, one twin was fairly dependent, sociable, and placid; the other was independent, diligent, and vigorous. Smith concludes that parental behavior was concerned with amplification and development of the differences between the twins, but the relative weight of importance of the behavioral differences and parental attitudes is unknown.

Psychologists suggest that parents respond to, rather than create, differences between their twins (Lytton 1980). In an observational study of 17 identical and 29 fraternal twins, they observed interactive behavior between parents and twins in the home and in an experimental situation. This study suggests that environmental impact is more important than genetics when it comes to "interaction." A reciprocal relationship was found to exist between parent and children, which Lytton believes is founded on real differences in twins rather than on parental perception of perceived differences.

However, clinicians (Allen, Greenspan, and Pollin 1976; Dibble and Cohen 1981) stress the importance of the parents' perception of their twin children in the development of personality. Although observable behavioral individuality is important, parental expectations have a life of their own that is not related to actual cues from the child. These clinicians agree that the process of differential perception and role delineation is part of a complex, overlapping interaction in which certain characteristics of the parents form a particular style of interaction between themselves and their twins. Within this interaction, specific characteristics of the parents lead them to focus on certain characteristics of the twin and respond to them systematically. Although difficult to observe, each twin learns to respond systematically to certain charac- teristics in each parent. The reciprocal relationships help to determine the personality of the child. Thus, these clinicians suggest that parents create differences between twins, based on their conscious and unconscious perceptions.

The issue of whether parents create personality differences in their twins or are responsive to them is the core question in twin development. For example, a mother and/or father may experience one of their twins as an independent and creative twin, while the other is experienced to be a more conforming and dependent twin. Such differences are in all likelihood, very minute. However, the mother must make these differentiations so as to be able to distinguish between her twins so that she can identify with each twin. We may speculate that the more emotionally healthy the mother, the more likely she is to respond to real differences between children rather than to create them. Furthermore, the twins themselves respond to the distinctions which mother makes between them. It is the nature of the twinship that generates the question, Which came first, the chicken or the egg? Although we do not have an answer for this question, herein lies the true fascination of twinship.

One of the authors (Schave 1982), looking at locus of control—e.g., internality-externality orientation in 6 year-old twins and their parents—suggests that not only do identical twins have different conceptions of their ability to control their world, but they also relate differently to their mother's locus of control. In this study each of the identical twins took on different aspects of the mother's internality-externality. This is one scientific piece of evidence to show that mothers identify with and differentiate between their twins. This reciprocal process helps the mother to form distinct relationships with each twin and assists the twins in developing as individuals.

Summing up the body of research on personality development in twins, it appears that behavioral psychologists ask questions about similarities in twin development, whereas clinicians, who are more individually oriented, seek out differences in twin development as they would in all persons. In reality there is limited developmental information pertaining to personality development in twins. Up to this point, we have not introduced the subject of the relationship between the twins. How does their relationship affect their growth as individuals? By looking at this question, we might indeed attain a better understanding of twin development.

THE
TWINNING
BOND

There is no precise definition of the *twinning bond*—perhaps it is beyond definition. Various descriptions of the twinning bond exist in the twin literature and depend on the perspective of the writer. It is clear, however, that the twinning bond begins at conception and continues consciously or unconsciously throughout the lives of the twins. This section describes what has been observed to be the twinning bond and reports the research to substantiate its existence.

The twinning bond has been described as a psychological thread between twins. It may manifest itself as a similar response to the environment and may include a heightened sense of telepathy or extrasensory perception. An accurate description of the twinning bond necessarily includes its development: Why do twins have a psychological thread that serves to connect them?

The most obvious reason for the existence of a bond between identical twins is their similar genetic and constitutional beginnings. Further, among identical and fraternal twins the impact of the environment and parental style serve to make their experiences very similar; thus their resultant responses are also very much alike. These genetic, constitutional, and environmentally similar experiences serve to establish very early in the twins' lives what has come to be called the twinning bond.

Another way of looking at the twinning bond is to see it as a mutual dependency between individuals. Tabor and Joseph (1961) defined *twinning* as follows:

> The twinning reaction consists of mutual interidentification and part fusion of the self representation and the objects representation of the other member of the pair. This leads to a difference of ego boundaries between two people. This reaction may occur in siblings who are relatively close together in age, or it may occur between couples married for a period of time. (p. 277)

In other words the twinning process involves experiencing oneself as part of the other person (i.e., the twin). A sense of self is shared or distributed between the individuals of the pair. This unconscious process of partially merged identities is often not considered unusual or disruptive to a young pair of twins. An illustration of partially merged identities is what other researchers have pointed out to be twin language (i.e., the use of *we* for *me*). The results of this shared identity lead to a special closeness—a sense of belonging to one another.

Although twins learn coexistence, socialization, and cooperation earlier than single children and they rarely suffer from loneliness as single children may, the problem of individuation remains critical (Scheinfield 1967). As noted in clinical studies, problems in identification and ego development may occur as a result of twinship (Burlingham 1952; Leonard 1961; Tabor and Joseph 1961). Identification, as defined by Hinsie and Campbell (1970), is

> the most primitive method of recognizing external reality; it is, in fact, nothing less than mental mimicry. Its necessary preconditions are unbroken narcissism, which cannot bear that anything should exist outside itself, and the weakness of the individual, which makes him unable to annihilate his environment or take flight from it. The child then uses identification to transform what is strange and frightening in the external world into what is familiar and enjoyable. (p. 373)

Identification between twins is usually mutually reciprocal and of equal intensity. This identification is made with an individual on the same level of development, instead of with an older sibling or an adult, which is what developmentally occurs in singletons. This identification between twins conflicts with the parental relationship. Further, the intertwin identification appears to have commenced so early that its origin is difficult to determine (Leonard 1961). We may speculate that identifications between twins have an effect upon their later achievements.

According to psychoanalytic theory, single children identify with the mother or primary caretaker and through this process become aware of their separateness. In the case of twins, each infant must go through identification and separation with the mother and with the twin (Leonard 1961). The relationship between infant twins is elusive and nonverbal, and there is a lack of differentiation that precedes awareness of body boundaries. Further, the need for the twin is different than the need for the mother, as the twin is experienced as part of the self in infancy. Maturation of sensory perception is necessary before one twin can begin to perceive himself/herself as separate from the other. Perhaps twin differentiation begins through touching and poking each other. Separation occurs more naturally from the mother, who already has attained her own sense of separateness from the child.

Gradually, a twin baby perceives that his/her twin is really another individual, not an extension of himself/herself or a mirror image. In early childhood there appears to be a continuum, never a sharp delineation, between a sense of oneness and the realization of separation. At this stage the primary intertwin identification resembles the primary identification with the mother in that it is based on play and ego gratification. The influence of the primary intertwin identification is evident in later stages of development and in some instances throughout the life of the twins.

Identification between twins often retards the maturation of both individuals, causing language difficulties and interference with the formation of object relationships. Just as the dependence on the mother prevents complete separation of the maternal self-images in the single child, the dependency of one twin on the other often causes self-images to remain blurred. This blurring of self-images leads to confusion in identity, which is one result of the primary intertwin identification. This primary intertwin identification may complicate the development of a healthy and separate ego. Some twins clearly show difficulty in separating the self from the nonself. However, continuation of the intertwin identification and lack of individuation do not in themselves lead to serious personality disturbances (Leonard 1961).

Burlingham (1952) has observed that twins who come from low socioeconomic backgrounds, with very similar physical appearances, and parental and cultural attitudes that do not stress individuation often do experience severe problems in language development and ego development.

Leonard has observed that lack of ego development is exemplified in retardation of twin language.

Farber's (1981) research, which relies on a psycho-dynamic point of view, theorizes that the twin bond is manifest as intrapsychic conflict between twins. She writes:

> Overall, the findings underscore the significance of individuality. If twins reared in even moderately different homes remain markedly alike, what more do we need in order to acknowledge the genetic uniqueness of each individual? Similarly, if twins make themselves "artificially" different as a result of contact with each other, what more do we need to indicate the need of each individual to be an individual, separate unto himself and clearly bounded! (p. 53)

Twinness, the closeness of the twins as seen by themselves and others, has been described and studied (Zazzo 1960). Vandenberg and Wilson (1979), inspired by Zazzo, constructed a 28-item questionnaire on twin closeness for mothers and twins and correlated the twin differences in scores on six Primary Mental Abilities subtests. They concluded that no evidence of a relationship between the twin situation and cognitive variables was apparent for identical and fraternal twins. These researchers suggested that the twin situation may influence personality development.

Paluszny and Gibson (1974) in a longitudinal study of 10 sets of middle-class fraternal twins of nursery-school age, analyzed the determinants of the twinning relationship. They found that five sets of twins showed some form of mutual dependency and two sets showed one-sided dependency. In each case mother-child dependency was excessive. These mothers had difficulties separating from their twins and actively encouraged them to be similar and dependent on each other. Three pairs showed minimal or no dependency. A follow-up study 6 years later revealed none of the twins had persistent problems with rivalry or mutual dependence. These researchers concluded that the twinning bond is transient and age specific in fraternal twins.

Paluszny and Beht-Hallahni (1974) explored the nature of the twinning bond by asking twins in their thirties how they would describe their twin, using the semantic differential. They found that all subjects rated their twin like the twin's own description. It was found that the twins who were the closest used more projection and did not marry, finding separation from the other twin too painful. This study indicates that the twinning bond is not transient and that it does effect adulthood.

In conclusion, although the twinning bond is elusive, its existence has been demonstrated by researchers as well as described by clinicians and twins. This bond affects personality development in twins but only becomes a pathological interaction when parents are of low socioeconomic status, when parents stress similarity and dependence in their twins, and when the parents' culture reinforces these actions.

PARENTAL INFLUENCES ON TWIN DEVELOPMENT

Appropriate parenting behaviors with twins have been a concern for parents, pediatricians, and clinicians. Although research on personality differences in twins clearly indicates that the parental role is a critical factor, research on the effect of parenting on twins is limited. Clinical speculation, based on pathological development in twins, and general speculation by parents, in addition to limited research on parenting twins, provides the extent of knowledge in this area.

Burlingham (1952) added to the clinical perspective of the literature on parenting twins. She observed that the first problem confronting the mother of twins, besides the physical demands of "double trouble," was developing a relationship with each twin. The more similar the twins are in appearance, the longer it takes the mother to distinguish between them and to make an attachment to them as separate individuals. Unit attachment usually precedes individual attachment and is further complicated by the fact that twin personalities change and switch during the first year of life. The mother often feels that it is a serious failing on her part, a lack of love, if she cannot distinguish between her twins. In reality she needs to be able to identify with them in order to love them.

This problem is less critical with fraternal twins, as they are less similar in appearance (Gromada 1981).

In many instances it is difficult for parents to give indentical twins individual treatment and opportunities even if it is in their philosophy of child rearing (Burlingham 1952). Advice to "develop individuality" in twins is often difficult to follow because twins want to dress alike, they are jealous of each other's possessions, and they do not like to be separated. Burlingham suggests:

> *Identical twins, when they grow up, often fail to develop into two separate human beings. It remains a matter of conjecture whether this is due to the twinship itself, or due to the attitude of the mother who in their infancy could not tell them apart; who was driven by an inner urge to give them the same opportunities and experiences, thus treating them as one being instead of two. (p. 52)*

Scheinfield (1967) argued that it is a grave error to try to bring up identical twins as if they were halves of the same person and to expect them always to be close to each other. Any forced relationship will threaten future development and should be avoided. However, to accept dogmatically one theory of child rearing—"individualize and separate"—for all twins is not realistic nor is it supported by research. The special relationship shared by twins should be respected by the parents and fostered. Similarities and differences will reveal themselves in abilities and interests as the twins develop. Although twins present special problems in individuation for parents, if they are raised with enough freedom to be themselves, later problems, as they relate to the twinship, are unlikely to occur.

Cohen, Dibble, and Grave (1977) and Lytton (1980) contend that parental behavior is the most important determinant of the child's socialization. Indeed, the remaining research studies on parenting twins suggest that environmental influences are primary determinants of the development of a sense of individual identity within twin pairs.

CONCLUSION   In concluding this chapter, several issues become apparent. Firstly, there is no agreement among researchers as to the relative importance of heredity as compared with environmental influences. Behavioral psychologists see similarities between identical twins. Clinicians see differences between identical twins. Juxtaposed with these insights is the suggestion that interaction between parents and twins and between the twins themselves critically affects personality growth and development. Finally, knowledge to date on twin development is limited owing to greater concern with issues focused on the nature-nurture controversy. It becomes our concern to look at twins as people with unique patterns of identity development.

2

IDENTITY FORMATION

Time present and time past
Are both perhaps present in time future,
And time future contained in time past.
                              T. S. Eliot

Identity formation is a major facet of most personality theories. The understanding of identity formation is very complex, with very few self-evident truths. For the present purpose, identity can be conceptualized as the interaction of the biological endowment, the dynamics of the family system, the givens of the childhood experience, and the impact of the social environment.

The function or purpose of identity is to give the individual a continuous sense of his own internal reality, which is constantly subject to change. The structure of identity then determines how the individual interacts with his environment. In other words, identity reflects the aspect of personality that is used to interact with the real world. Some aspects of identity are implicit because they were developed

---

The epigraph is taken from *Burnt Norton,* in "Four Quartets," copyright 1943 by T.S. Eliot; renewed 1971 Esme Valerie Eliot. Reprinted by permission of Harcourt Brace Jovanovich, Inc.

in infancy and early childhood and thus may have been determined unconsciously. Explicit aspects of identity are more consciously chosen as the individual matures. How the individual deals with emotions [affects] is a central aspect of identity that affects ego functioning, including one's thought processes.

Identity formation is developmental with expectable behaviors being appropriate to certain ages. Thus a clearer understanding of identity includes a developmental perspective. The theories of child development that were chosen in this chapter provide clear and striking descriptions of identity formation. Erikson's theory of psychosocial development is presented first. Second, Harry Stack Sullivan's interpersonal psychology is explained. Next, Margaret Mahler's crucial theory of the process of separation-individuation is described. Finally, Piaget's theory is delineated to help elucidate that part of personality that is determined by cognition. All of these theories contribute to the formulation of a comprehensive theory of identity formation.

ERIK   Erik Erikson, in *Identity: Youth and*
ERIKSON   *Crisis* (1968), harkens back to the
Jamesian view of identity. William James (1922) wrote:

> *A man's character is discernible in the mental or moral attitude [identity] in which, when it came upon him, he felt himself most deeply and intensely active and alive. At such moments there is a voice inside which speaks and says: "This is the real me!" . . . an element of active tension, of holding my own, as it were, and trusting outward things to perform their part so as to make it a full harmony, but without any guarantee that they will. Make it a guarantee . . . and the attitude immediately becomes to my consciousness stagnant and stingless. Take away the guaranty, and I feel a sort of deep enthusiastic bliss, of bitter willingness to do and suffer anything . . . and which, although it is a mere mood or emotion to which I can give no form in words, authenticates itself to me as the deepest principle of all active and theoretic determination which I possess. (p. 199)*

Incorporating both this subjective sense and descriptive perception of identity with a theoretical framework of child development, Erikson's contributions are unique. Erikson's expansion of psychoanalytic theory is founded in the area of ego formation or that part of one's personality that functions in relation to reality experiences. A theory of child develop- ment is central to personality formation from Erikson's point of view. The focus of this psychosocial theory is the develop- ment of identity within the context of the family as well as the culture.

Erikson saw the individual progressing through eight stages of development from infancy to old age (Erickson 1950). These stages are dependent upon each other in the sense that the tasks of each stage must be completed or else they interfere with the individual's healthy progression toward identity formation. A task that is not resolved at a particular stage will manifest itself as a conflict later in the individual's life.

Basic trust vs. basic mistrust is Erikson's first develop- mental stage and thus the foundation of one's ego strength and vital personality development. From a state of inner biological and physical tension created by the need for eating, sleeping, and eliminating, the infant gradually comes to develop expectations from his environment that his caretakers will meet his needs. As the infant becomes more familiar with the positive feelings associated with comfort, he is increasingly able to be adventuresome about his new feelings and environment, including people other than mother (the primary caretaker). In other words, good feelings become predictable and are generally associated with the mother's presence. If the infant's fundamental physical requirements are not responded to properly, the infant becomes mistrustful of his environment and begins to become apprehensive, untrusting, or fearful of encounters with his world. Erikson (1950) states:

> *Such consistency, continuity, and sameness of experience provide a rudimentary sense of ego identity which depends, I think, on the recognition that there is an inner population of remembered and anticipated sensations and images which are*

firmly correlated with the outer population of familiar and predictable things and people. (p. 147)

Later in this first stage, the mother will begin to set limits for her child in relation to what is permissible and what is prohibited. No absolute amount of time, food, or material objects is important. It is the quality of the relationship between mother and child that extends the trust between them and encourages psychological growth, which is the basis of identity formation. The specific task of identity development at this earliest stage, according to Erikson, is: "I am what hope I have and give" (Erikson 1968).

Erikson's second developmental stage, *autonomy vs. shame and doubt,* begins in the second year of life. It is in this stage that the highly dependent child begins to experience his autonomous will, asserting himself with his family. For the child to work through this stage successfully, he must be treated with dignity and respect. His capacity for independence must be fostered by parents who believe their child is capable of independence, and thus are able to instill self-confidence in their child. At the same time, the parents must set limits for the child to ensure his safety and thus make him aware of his range of abilities and limits.

Parents who treat their child with respect and reassurance foster the development of self-control. Parents who doubt the child and are fearful of his independence create doubt and shame in the child, who then does not learn to trust his own abilities. Erikson (1950) writes:

> *From a sense of self control without loss of self esteem comes a clearer sense of good will and pride; from a sense of loss of self control and of foreign overcontrol comes a lasting propensity for doubt and shame. (p. 254)*

The crisis of the will at this stage leaves in the child the feeling that "I am what I can will freely" (Erikson 1968). Later, this first emancipation will be played out as a part of identity formation as the individual attempts to be independent and to choose and guide his own future.

Beginning in the third year of life through the fifth year, the child progresses through the stage of *initiative vs. guilt*. The child begins to see himself as a person in his own right and begins to trust his potential capacities.

Initiative adds to autonomy the quality of mastery and planning—the willful quality of the earlier stage is subdued. The child learns to moderate his behavior to delay, accomodate, and cooperate with others. Consequently, the child has to learn to draw the line between giving up his initiative through passivity or feeling guilt for going too far.

Parallel biological developments are taking place: the child is moving about on his own and encountering a wide range of new situations, and his comprehension and language development lead him to understand enough to pose numerous questions. Both of these developments lead to a new breadth of imaginary experiences. In psychological terms, cognitive advancement is also occurring and contributes profoundly to his sense of initiative.

An early sense of roles is also apparent. At this stage (3-5 years), the child begins to understand that he can affect changes in his environment by actively and aggressively intruding into his space and directing his activities toward other persons. This lays the groundwork for gender role identification and the early stages of what Freud described to be the Oedipus Complex. The child forms a romantic relationship with the parent of the opposite sex. The resolution of this childhood attachment to the father or the mother winds its way into the fabric of the individual's adult relationships. Within this stage the child comes to learn the expectations that his parents place on his behavior.

He may also experience the sweet success of appropriate acceptance as a loving and lovable child and thus be able to act on his own initiative later in life. If the child is indulged and allowed to experience too threatening an amount of sexual gratification, he will become guilty, which will affect his later sexual development. If parents are punitive and unaccepting of the child's emergent sexual feeling, the same outcome can be predicted. Of course, much of the child's sexual gratification is experienced in fantasy.

It is at this stage that parents are challenged to set limits and also to direct appreciation toward the child for these most significant feelings. "I am what I imagine I can be" is the identity gain of this stage (Erikson 1968).

The next developmental stage from roughly 6-11 years is referred to as *latency* by Freudians and as the stage of a sense of *industry vs. inferiority* by Erikson. The main goal for the child at this stage is to gain a sense of competence and a feeling that he can be productive—"a rudimentary parent," even though the biological parent will be dormant to him for years to come.

The child learns to gain recognition through learning and production. He adjusts himself to the world of "tools." The danger of this stage is a sense of inadequacy and inferiority. Such a result can be the product of the child's insufficient preparation for this productive stage. The child may still prefer to take on the "baby role".

This stage is socially decisive, i.e., the child is for the first time very involved with his peers as well as with his family. Success and failure are foremost in the child's experience at this point. Competence from the peer group's point of view is critical because the child measures himself against the standard of his peers as well as against his parents' expectations.

Learning to overcome feelings of failure and to work effectively in a group is the basis for effective mastery of learning and work in later life. The specific task of identity development at this stage is: "I am what I can learn to make work."

The next stage, which brings about the termination of childhood and ushers in adolescence, is *identity vs. role confusion*. This stage covers what is otherwise understood to be adolescence. Mainly the task at hand is to achieve an integration of ego development from all of the earlier stages with a resurgence of instinctual energies added to the task. Erikson states (1950) that

> the emphasis in peer group identification is different from the previous stage. An individual takes on or assumes qualities of a particular group or individual that he can identify with and

project his feeling on to. This process allows the individual to gradually clarify his own sense of identity in both personal and career aspects of life. (p. 161)

In this search for identity, the mind of the adolescent is filled with ideologies that are in part based on the morality learned by the child and the ethical demands of adulthood. The adolescent seeks out career identification as well as sexual identifications. Role confusion is the product of the adolescent's inability to identify adequately with others.

The search for intimacy is the first major task the individual faces after his quest for identity. Intimacy, according to Erikson, is the capacity to commit oneself to concrete affiliation and partnerships and to have the tenacity to pursue them even though they demand sacrifices and compromises of the previous-gained identity. At this point in life Erikson believes that it is healthy or adaptive for the individual to want to fuse or merge his sense of self with others.

True sexuality can develop fully at this stage. At earlier stages of sexual development, it was merely self-seeking and could not involve the self-abandon of the intimate relationship.

Isolation, the avoidance of contacts that commit to intimacy, is the counterpart of intimacy. The need of the isolated individual is to destroy forces and people whose presence invades his space or territory. Intimacy and competition are too overwhelming to the individual who must choose isolation to avoid fusion, conflict, and love. The growth of the individual at this stage is: "We are what we love."

The stage of *generativity vs. stagnation* is reached in adulthood. *Generativity* is the concern for guiding the next generation. It is the role of the adult to raise children and to function as a productive and creative individual. Altruism is another form of generativity and in that sense may absorb the same kind of drive from which parental energy evolves.

A sense of stagnation or boredom is a regression to an obsessive need for pseudointimacy, a concern for oneself as when one was a child, and involvement with stereotypical identity. Stagnation grows out of a lack of expansion or enrichment of ego interests, which is rooted in earlier life stages.

Ego integrity vs. despair is Erikson's final stage of development. Integrity involves the individual's accrued sense of meanings. The individual can accept his life and the people in it who have been significant without the wish that things should have been different. Integrity also indicates that one's life is one's own responsibility.

The lack or loss of an accrued ego integration is labeled *despair.* A lack of hope and sometimes a feeling of contempt and displeasure are part of the experience of despair for the individual who feels that there is not time to start a new life or begin on a new path to ego integration.

In conclusion, Erikson's psychosocial theory provides a framework for an understanding of identity formatioll. Indeed, identity is the concept upon which the path of personality development proceeds in this theory. Identity as presented by Erikson is not so much the identity concerned with individual difference as it is that concerned with social cultural identity. In a sense he was a pioneer of the significance of social experiences upon ego development. He enriched or broadened psychoanalytic theory to include the impact of culture and society, while maintaining the significance of parenting on the development of identity. Because Erikson's theory concerns itself with identity formation, it is useful for our own purposes, although its clinical and scientific usefulness may be limited.

The application of Eriksonian theory to twin development is speculative. However, the first obvious discrepancy between the development of a single child through Eriksonian stages and twin development is found in the first stage of trust vs. mistrust. Twins have a different relationship with the mother because they are two rather than one. The quality of time, both physical and emotional, that the mother spends with each child is different from that which she would spend if she had one child. This is the first critical determinant of twin development that is different from that of single children.

Another obvious difference in twin development is the continual presence of the twin sibling. If the twin infant develops a different kind of bond with the mother than a single child, he or she has the bond with the twin as a compensation. This bond begins in the first stage of life and continues throughout the lives of the twins. The bond between twins can be described as primary along with the mother-child bond. It begins before the mother-child bond or at the same time as the primary attachment to the mother in the first stage of development (trust vs. mistrust).

The unique bonding of twins to the mother and to each other colors the second stage of life. The experience of willfulness at this stage is distorted as the twins keep their dependence on one another, while at the same time protesting against authority. Perhaps it is harder for the mother to set limits against this dynamic duo, or perhaps the mother sets firmer limits for her twins because things seem to need more control. At this toddler stage twins may and may not experience the autonomy that single children do. It is clear, however, that they do not have the independence of the single child. They may grow appropriately independent of the mother, but there is no mechanism that we know of that will help them grow apart from one another.

Twins may enter the third stage of development with confusion as to who is who. There is most likely a merging of egos because of the twin bond and because of the lack of independence from one another as toddlers. It is apparent then that the twin child is going to have a harder time knowing who he is and trusting his capabilities. If the parents do not make distinctions between their twins, it is at this point that the twins begin to create differences between themselves to complete this stage of development. This creation of differences or even parental distinctions may be overdetermined in ways which place one twin in one role and the other twin in an opposite role. At any rate it seems that competition between the twins for parental attention is appropriate at this stage. Such competition will exist except in situations where twins have merged their identities.

Twins gain a sense of competence together. They compare themselves with each other and set standards for one another. The development of separate interests and abilities, which is crucial at this stage, is highly dependent on parenting. When parenting is less than optimal, twins gain either no sense of separate competence or they compensate for one another with one twin excelling in one area, while the other twin excels in another area. Unit identity, the partial merging of egos, becomes apparent in some twins at this stage. Unit identity decreases the twins' need for appropriate other peer relationships outside of the twinship.

Entrance into adolescence is oftentimes not as traumatic for twins as for single children. The intertwin identification is strong, and thus the need for other identifications is minimized and also agreed upon by the twin pair. Twins do not suffer the loneliness and anxiety in their search for identity if the bond between them is highly interdependent.

The crisis of intimacy is entirely different for twins, who are born as partners. At this stage of life, twins may choose to keep their own intimate relationship as the central one in their lives, or they may separate and find other relationships difficult. The need for affiliation may be denied completely, or it may be overdetermined in young adulthood.

As Erikson's last stages are determined existentially, it is hard to predict in general how twins will relate to parenting and ego integrity. Certainly these aspects of identity will be colored by the roots of their identity, which are to be found in the twinship.

HARRY STACK SULLIVAN

Harry Stack Sullivan's (1953) theory of interpersonal psychiatry was influenced by Freudian theory, psychobiologic therapy, humanistic psychiatry, and his own vast clinical experiences with schizophrenia as well as neurosis. Sullivan saw the primary concern of psychiatry as the study of interpersonal relationships. Sullivan was the first psychiatrist to point out that interpersonal relationships involve more than what goes on between two or more people (Harper 1959).

Sullivan's theory of interpersonal relationships includes the relationships an individual might have with imaginary people (i.e., the perfect lover or perfect friend) or with illusions of personification (i.e., idealization of a childhood friend, brother, or sister). A *parataxic distortion* was Sullivan's term for an individual experience related to fantasy or an idealization within the interpersonal situation instead of the existent reality. For example, when a twin is separated from his sibling for the first time, he frequently expects that all other relationships will be similar to his relationship with his brother or sister. Parataxic distortions keep people from making secure and satisfying interpersonal relationships (Sullivan 1953).

Sullivan saw the purpose of human behavior as being twofold. First, he believed that individuals pursue satisfaction through meeting the biological needs for sex, food, and sleep. The second purpose of life is the pursuit of human closeness and security, which is related to the first set of needs but is harder to achieve. This more complicated purpose includes a sense of acceptance and of belonging to a group.

For Sullivan the process of becoming human was the process of socialization. Before the child is aware of separateness, the attitudes of the mother are conveyed to the child through empathy—the transference of the mother's feelings onto the child. If the mother is anxious, the child senses this anxiety, which is transferred back to the child. Thus the first sense of feeling—whether it be anxiety or whether it be security—is transferred from the mother.

The degree of anxiety or the degree of security which is transferred contributes to the development of the self and to the evolution of types of parataxic distortions. Interpersonal relationships will in all cases determine psychological well-being. The way that significant others value the child will affect self-perception. If parents value the child, he will feel worthy of love; if they devalue the child, he will grow up without self-love.

Sullivan saw the infant as having three self-personifications. First, there is the "good me," which contains secure feelings. The "bad me" contains states of anxiety. Finally, the "not me" contains primitive anxiety including uncanny horror and fear that is only apparent in psychosis and nightmares.

As in Eriksonian theory, the infant develops through stages that have different milestones. Failure to complete a stage successfully will leave the individual fixated at this stage. In other words, completion of one stage is contingent upon completion of the earlier stage.

The first stage in Sullivan's theory is *infancy*. This stage lasts from birth to the time of articulate speech. During this stage the mother's attitude and nourishment of the child's psychological and physical well-being are critical. From this stage the developing infant receives his/her basic sense of self-worth.

The following stage, *childhood*, begins with the development of language, which expresses the beginning of a capacity for communication and thus is a critical aspect of self-development. While developing his interpersonal skills, the child must also learn to control some of the behaviors that were tolerated in the earlier stage of infancy.

The *juvenile era* commences when the child has a need for peers. Through the experience of schooling, the child is exposed to broader aspects of life. At this same time the self is developing and the child is learning the value of competition, cooperation, and compromise.

Preadolescence, which extends from 8-12 years, is characterized by the capacity to love and to develop relationships. Sullivan stresses the importance of the intimacy of two chums in this stage. Through communication developed with peers, such personal inadequacies carried over from previous stages can be alleviated or overcome.

Adolescence is the period of turmoil and emotionality. It is at this stage that the youth establishes relationships with the opposite sex for personal and social gratification. If the self-system has not matured adequately, personality problems are manifested as inadequate and inappropriate personifications of the self. Adolescents with "warped" self-concepts are unable to grasp the fact that their personifications of themselves are distorted. Sullivan felt that adolescents with a warped self-concept are unable to gain insight into themselves since such insight stirs up anxiety that has been previously repressed.

Maturity will contain the achievements of each developmental era. The mature person will be able to relate intimately with other persons and will have insight into how to instigate meaningful interpersonal relationships.

Sullivan's theory is unique and significant because of the emphasis he placed on interpersonal interactions. Intimacy, which is for Sullivan the sign of maturity, is particularly relevant to twin development. Do twins, because of their shared experiences, develop an ability to be intimate sooner than single children? Is it possible that intimacy, with others develops later in twins than in single children?

We may speculate that the first stage of development—the growth of the empathic relationship with mother—is augmented by the presence of a twin sibling. The bond between twins is highly empathic in nature, perhaps providing twins with more experiences of closeness in infancy. The childhood stage that focuses on language and communication may be enriched by the presence of a twin sibling who adds a nonverbal and more playful quality to the development of communication.

However, the closeness between twins and their ability to communicate nonverbally become a problem in the juvenile era. Twins, because they have each other, can combat the influence of the schooling experience by remaining exclusive with one another. Most likely, they have already learned competition, compromise, and cooperation at an earlier stage, and so they do not feel so compelled to relearn this lesson with peers.

In preadolescence the twins are each other's best friends, even if other friends are sought out. By this stage they have agreed upon their parataxic distortions of each other and therefore cannot help each other overcome feelings of inadequacy. Roles in relationship to one another are fixed. Clearly, this is a problem for those twins who do not have the stimulation of others to help them understand the meaning of social interaction outside of the twinship.

Twins confront adolescence together. Their adolescence is not as conflicted, nor is it as growth oriented socially as it is for single adolescents. In most cases reliance on one another will limit the chances of other social interactions and the knowledge and experience that go along with other commitments.

It is not unusual for twins to enter maturity without sufficiently broad experiences of social interaction. Yet twins can be quite comfortable with intimacy. In fact the early dose of empathy allows twins to seek out intimacy without a diversified knowledge of interpersonal relationships.

Twins often need to go back and experience social interactions that are less intense than their twin interactions. Whether they choose to relate to others in the intense fashion of twinship is a choice that should be made after they learn to relate on a more superficial level. Sullivan's theory clarifies some of the problems of twinship: Is always having a best buddy the best of all situations? How do twins learn to enjoy being alone? How much intimacy is appropriate in a relationship? Where should sharing and caring stop?

MARGARET   Margaret Mahler (1967), a psycho-
MAHLER   analyst, describes the psychological
birth of the human infant. The stages of development leading to an acquisition of a sense of self—a sense of identity separate from the mother—are carefully delineated by this theorist and researcher. The primary concern of Mahler's research is to show how normal children separate their self-images from the images of the mother. Her descriptions of how the child moves from oneness to separateness are based on direct observations of the preverbal mother-child interaction. Kaplan (1978) states:

> *In the end, Mahler discovered the process that begins the shaping of a human being. When this process goes wrong, a human being will have difficulties loving others, nurturing the young, taming his own aggression, knowing the boundaries of immediate time and space, mourning the dead, and caring about the destiny of human beings. (p. 17)*

Mahler theorizes that the mother's psychological history will influence her infant's development of selfhood. The mother's impressions of her child are shaped by her conscious and unconscious fantasies as well as by the baby's characteristics. The father's fantasies and interactions also affect the child's development of separateness.

The first phase of separation-individuation from birth to 1 month is the *autistic phase* (Mahler 1968). The child is primarily concerned with his bodily functions. Phase two from 2-6 months is labeled the *symbiotic phase*. The mother and child are psychologically still one. The mother through her own ability to empathize with her child's cues for physical and emotional comfort protects the child from the new environment. The child is deeply affected by the care he receives from his mother. The critical determinant of successful resolution of this stage is the mother's ability to respond to the child's needs. Infants who must shape their behavior to meet their mother's needs will fail to establish adequate me/not me perceptions (i.e., ego boundaries).

Mahler postulates that the child progresses through the separation-individuation substages at his own rate and that substages overlap into one another. After 4 months the child begins to break away from symbiotic fusion with the mother. The *differentiation subphase* from approximately 4-10 months is characterized by the child's growing self-awareness and goal-directed activity. The child begins to differentiate between the mother and others. Stranger anxiety appears at the end of this subphase.

The *early practicing subphase* from 10-12 months includes the child's recognition of his own body parts. At this phase the child has the ability to play alone as long as the mother is nearby. However, when the mother is gone, the infant's activity level drops.

The *practicing subphase* proper from 12-15 months includes the child's pleasure over mastery of locomotion and other independent activities. As independent as the child seems, when the mother leaves the room, the child slows down his activity until the mother returns. The mother's approval is most crucial to the child at this stage. The mother must encourage the child's independence. By her availability as well as by her intermittent absences, the mother fosters the child's gratification in his independent efforts.

The *rapprochment subphase* from 15-24 months includes the child's growing awareness of others and a need to recognize and relate to them. Mahler does not label this stage "autonomy," but the process she describes—the ability to separate and to individuate while checking back with the mother, who is taking pride in her child's accomplishments—is similar to the Eriksonian stage of autonomy vs. shame.

Through the use of words and exploration of the environment, by 3 years of age, the child who has successfully separated from the mother will have attained object constancy or object permanence in Piagetian terms. He will have a mental picture of the mother as separate and individual from himself. Thus ego boundaries are clearly defined and are contingent upon the manner in which the parents have viewed and treated the child. A child who has been accepted for both positive and negative attributes will be able to accept himself. A child who has not been valued will be unable to accept any positive aspects of himself. A child who has been accepted unconditionally will be unable to understand limits.

As in the theory postulated by Sullivan, Mahler states that empathic relationships are based upon a relationship with the mother. For twins it is probable that to some degree empathy is also developed as a result of the twin relationship. This is speculative and a difficult concept to demonstrate. It is probable that the twin relationship may contribute to an ever-present amount of empathy between twins and a tendency for twins to be empathic in other relationships.

Mahler's separation-individuation theory is a model for what occurs between mothers and children. Are there ways in which this model is useful in understanding how twins evolve to the stage of separating from one another? Furthermore, when does separation occur between twins? It appears that separation from one's twin is contingent upon the nature of the mothering experience for the twins. There may be a variety of types of experiences related to separation that twins go through on their paths to individuality.

The siginificance of this psychological theory of identity formation is that through Mahler's research we are clear about the importance of the mother's psychological interactions with her child. With respect to the mother's interactions with twin children, it may be that she interacts differently with each twin based upon her own individual psychological state.

JEAN PIAGET   Jean Piaget (1950), a genetic epistemologist and developmental psychologist, was concerned with tracing the development of human intelligence. To understand the development of the thought processes, Piaget asked ingenious questions that provide empirical evidence on the development of cognition from birth through adolescence. Piaget described cognitive development as stagelike, a progression which is continuous and irreversible from sensorimotor learning to formal operational thought. As the individual progresses through these stages, previous understanding is transformed into new comprehension. The child asks different questions about the environment, which leads to new answers and new understanding.

Although Piaget viewed development as fundamentally determined by biology, he saw social realities as determinants of the environment that could bolster the availability and variation of cognition. That is, Piaget envisioned the environment as providing enriching opportunities for promoting cognitive development. On the other hand, the environment can constrict the child's experiences so that development will not proceed on a normal course (Cowan 1978). Piagetian research has shown that not all adults attain formal operation, which may be due to emotional as well as environmental deprivation (Elkind 1970, Flavell 1963, Muss 1982). Piaget inadvertently connects the affective with the cognitive aspects of personality development by describing social cognition. Flavell (1963) has called Piaget the father of social cognition.

According to Piaget, the *sensorimotor stage* begins at birth and continues until approximately 2 years of age. In this early stage the infant learns through his senses: touching, feeling, sucking, and seeing. The infant lacks an ability to differentiate between himself and the larger world. As sensorimotor coordination becomes more complex, including social attachment, a resulting differential between the self and others as social beings is accomplished.

There are six substages of sensorimotor development. The first substage includes the emergence of directed behavior (0-1½ months), which is the basis of primary emotions and cognition. There is an absence of permanent schemes (memory). Once the parents leave the perceptual field, they are gone from the infant memory.

The second substage includes the beginning coordination of sensorimotor schemes (memory, 2-4 months). The infant looks to see and moves to look. He reacts responsively to people as interesting objects, but there is no true social interaction.

The beginning of intentional activity from 4-6 months is the third substage. The infant follows objects as they disappear from view but then abandons the search. The infant begins to be fascinated with social objects and may cry when the parent leaves the room. However, Piaget says that at this stage there is no memory of the parent. This description of infant memory contradicts the Freudian and neo-Freudian view that the child at this stage has a strong attachment to the mother.

Substage four from 6-12 months includes the growth of the notion that there are objects that exist even when they are not in view. The infant's entrance into the world of objects is still shaky. Infants at this stage can distinguish between caretakers—thus more intense pleasure or frustration is experienced directly in relation to the caretaker. Cowan (1978) writes:

> For Piaget, the development of attachment is not simply a change in direction of affective energy. It represents instead a restructuring of the whole cognitive and affective universe as objects become permanent, people take on permanent existence in the child's mind. . . . The construction of attachment to caretakers, then, grows out of a matrix of changes in which there is reciprocal development in conception of the physical world, the social world and the self. (p. 96)

The fifth substage from 12-18 months involves the toddler's search for knowledge through trial and error, a never-ending quest for scientific discovery. As the toddler becomes aware of his success and failures in the world, he expands his interests in other social relationships.

The end of sensorimotor learning is from 18 months to 2 years. The toddler has learned to distinguish between action and representations. Language is used for communication, which has limited meaning to others but extends sociability. The complete transformation to mental symbols and the explosion of spoken language occur in the preoperational stage.

During the sensorimotor stage the child believes that his sensory impressions are essential to the existence of the objects. The child cannot separate his actions from other people or other objects until object permanence is attained. Sensorimotor learning establishes that concepts are not equivalent to words. Thought precedes language, which is based on the sensorimotor play and imitations of this first stage.

During *preoperation* from 2-7 years, language development and the ability to conceptualize are stabilized. Beginning reasoning is learned. Egocentrism (seeing the world from the child's point of view) declines, and play is used for ego development and definition.

At this stage the child accepts things as they seem to be and focuses on what is important to him. He excludes certain aspects of the task that do not interest him personally. The child learns to identify permanent qualities of objects and to predict changes and causality. Prelogic prevails in early childhood. The child absorbs, transmits, and communicates his own language and symbols. Therefore, control of thought processes goes from the internal state to the external state.

All of the child's learning is centered on his perceptions, which are egocentric. The child believes that everybody shares his perceptions and feelings about the world. Moral judgments are based on the perceived seriousness of the crime, not on the reality of the misdeed. Language functions to communicate the feelings of the child. Cooperation and the child's ability to understand others are the culminations of this stage.

Concrete operations from 7-11 years corresponds with latency in Freudian theory and industry vs. inferiority in Eriksonian theory and is the beginning of the ability to think hypothetically. The child can distinguish between appearance and reality. His judgments are based on the evaluation of the task at hand, not on his point of view. In this stage the child understands properties of measurement, including numbers as well as spatial properties.

Although children at this stage can advance concrete, logical hypotheses about reality, they do not realize that hypotheses are not necessarily facts. When they produce a mental construct, they believe that their thinking is real rather than just thinking.

Social and moral growth are advanced during this stage. The child can cooperate in a group, understanding his peer's point of view. He can reason and understand motivations in moral judgments. Involvement in personal accomplishments within the child's school is the task at hand. There is little interest in the world outside of the child's comprehension or hypothetical thinking. The child, in concrete operational thinking, begins with reality and moves reluctantly, if at all, to possibility.

The major cognitive task of *formal operations* (12 years-adulthood) is mastery of thought processes that are logical and abstract. The adolescent begins with possibilities and proceeds to reality. He suggests systems of thought and tests their reality and efficiency. Formal operational thinking is characterized by two abilities: (1) the ability to think abstractly and (2) the ability to recognize possibilities as well as actualities.

During adolescence a heightened sense of consciousness of themselves and of others is developed. Piaget and Inhelder (1969) state:

> *The adolescent not only tries to adapt his ego to the social environment but also emphatically tries to adjust the environment to his ego.... The result is a relative failure to distinguish between his own point of view and the point of view of the group. (p. 343)*

The adolescent becomes concerned with how others view him to the extent that he often loses his own point of view to that of the group. Piaget concurs with Erikson's idealism of adolescence and suggests that the adolescent believes that the world should submit itself to his highly idealistic thought process (how things should be) rather than the reality of how things are. Moral development can be extended and personality elaborated. Because of idealistic dreams, adolescents are often effective in bringing about change in society.

In conclusion, the more advanced the Piagetian stage, the more difficult it is for the individual to attain. Perhaps individuals only think abstractly in areas, where thoughts and feelings are integrated.

Eriksonian theory and Piagetian theory are complimentary. Although critics of Piaget claim that the theory is hard to operationalize, it is quite useful for enhancing our understanding of identity formation. It is our feeling that the impact of twinship on the stages of cognitive development is generally enriching for the twins. Their social sphere is expanded by each other. Adventures in the world are aided by each other. The social environment—including stable experiences with people in the environment—is enriched in comparison with single children.

In infancy the twin develops two strong attachments, one to the mother and one to the twin sibling. This serves to foster object permanence, the basis of all cognitive development. During preoperations (2-6 years) twins must deal with each other's perception, and each must therefore evaluate the validity of such perception, which also extends cognitive processes. Concrete operations and formal operations are also enriched by the close presence of another person, such as the presence of a twin sibling.

Indeed, cognitive development, according to Piaget, is enhanced by the presence of the twin sibling. Further, cognitive development does not cause different developmental problems for twins as compared with single children. It seems fair to predict that twins will develop cognitively at least at the same rate as single children.

CONCLUSION   The four theories presented and reviewed in relationship to identity formation and twin development are similar in that they conceptualize the development of identity as a process that begins at birth and that is affected by parenting and the social and cultural environment. However, these theorists also describe different aspects of the development of identity, which broadens one's understanding of identity formation.

Our point in presenting these theories is to show that identity formation in twins is different from identity formation in single children. Clearly, there are positive and negative aspects of twinship in relationship to identity formation. The crucial question is, What positive adaptations can be made by twins from the identity that they evolve from being twins? Conversely, What are the problems or drawbacks of twinship that can be addressed by twins, parents, teachers, and mental health professionals in an attempt to develop individuality in twins without destroying the special closeness of the twinship? The following chapters will describe our interviews with adult twins and the information that was collected and synthesized. In speaking with twins we kept in mind the problems that we saw twins confronting as well as the positive aspects of twinship.

3

CONVERSATIONS WITH ADULT TWINS

Behavioral geneticists (Floderus-Myhred et al. 1980; Gessell 1941; Scarr-Salaptik 1973) and educational psychologists (Brody and Brody 1976; Plomin and Rowe 1977; Wilson 1977) have investigated similarities between twins on measures of intelligence, cognitive development, measurable personality characteristics, physical attributes, and disease components, using sophisticated statistical measures to understand the genetic characteristics of identical and fraternal twins. Psychoanalytic clinicians (Hift 1980) have analyzed case histories of twin patients in an attempt to identify the psychopathology of the twinship and thereby prescribe precautionary measures for the healthy emotional development of twins. Ethnographic researchers (Lytton Conway & Suave 1977; Smith 1976) have attempted to observe the complexity of the parent-child interaction using twin subjects. Recently, a statistical reanalysis of case histories of identical twins reared apart speculates that differences between twins are a function of the interaction between the twins themselves in their search for individuality (Farber 1981).

One of the authors (Schave 1982) integrated the methods and findings of the above research designs and looked for similarities as well as differences between identical and fraternal twins and their parents on social aspects of self-development (locus of control and moral development). In this study both similarities and differences were found between the subjects. Her findings agree with Burlingham (1952),

41

indicating that the mother does indeed need to make distinctions between her identical twins to differentiate and to identify with them. This study also suggests that twins create differences between themselves as Farber (1981) speculated.

From the conclusions of this research, it became apparent that statistical measurements and clinical speculations about twin development, including the nature of the mother-child interaction and the twinning bond, were not clarifying the development of twin identity but, instead, were merely measuring manifestations of personality. Indeed, measurements of discrete personality variables are not indicative of what affected their development. Clinical material, although of greater depth, is limited to pathological development in twins.

The authors agreed that new knowledge would be gained by employing a different methodology. The methodology, an open-ended psychodynamic interview with twins who perceived themselves as successful and who were described as successful by their peers, was chosen. In employing this methodology the authors believed that they would have the optimum possibility of understanding the development of identity in twins, without the use of standarized personality tests or contrived questionaires.

PROCEDURE   The interviews were structured theoretically from the child development literature and twin research. The questions focused on issues of identity and intimacy, exploring these twin subjects' unique experiences, thoughts, and feelings about their twinship. What was it like for twins to grow up as twins? What are their thoughts and feelings now that they are adults? How did they see the twinship as affecting their identity? What was the quality of their relationships outside of their twinship? Could they describe some special feeling or bond between themselves and their twin?

The authors arranged to interview twins who were interested in the research project, twins who were willing to think about their twinships and twins who were motivated enough to participate in 1 to 2-hour interviews. Interviews were arranged at the convenience of the twin subjects. Each twin was interviewed separately. Both of the authors were present at each interview to gain agreement on the meaning of the data collected.

THE SAMPLE   The primary criterion that was established for the sample was that the twins interviewed perceived themselves as successful in most areas of their lives. Twins were located through informal social networks. Colleagues and friends were asked to suggest intelligent and articulate twins that they would be able to contact and to refer to the authors. Avoidance of advertising for twins or circulating interest more broadly was part of the procedure, as attracting twins whose strongest sense of identity was their twinship was considered counterproductive to the theoretical rationale of the study. The authors interviewed 20 sets of identical twins and 20 sets of fraternal twins from urban areas in the United States.

By broad and general standards, all of the twins interviewed were successful in their careers and had adequate relationships with other people. They were generally healthy, well-functioning individuals. Professions that were represented in this sample included medical doctors, psychiatrists, psychologists, academicians, social workers, writers, artists, musicians, lawyers, accountants, teachers, directors, interior decorators, dancers, a police officer, administrative assistants, and businessmen.

THE   Although the interviews were
INTERVIEWS   informal, specific topics were covered in each interview. Furthermore, the topics related to the development of identity and our knowledge of the psychological research on twins. There was no established order for these conversations. Interestingly, while speaking spontaneously, some of the participants covered a good many topics that were to be covered, while other twins had to be asked more specific questions.

The interviews covered 10 very broad topics. The first question posed was open-ended and unobtrusive to encourage free association and thus allow the participant freedom to choose where he/she would like to begin. The question was: "What is your earliest memory of the twinship?" The authors speculated that this earliest recollection of the twinship would be symbolic of the nature of their relationship with their twin.

As child development theory, as well as twin research, stresses the importance of parental interaction, the following areas of questioning were considered significant: "What were parental attitudes toward the twinship?" "How did your parents make distinctions between you and your twin?" "Were there any siblings in your family, and how did they react to the birth of twins?" "What was your parent's socioeconomic status?" "What were your parents' occupations?" Our sense was that the family environment and its attitude toward the twins would be an important determinant of early childhood development and later accomplishments in life.

Exploration of the early years of the twin relationship to the degree that they could be recalled was focused upon. The first issue in early childhood that was investigated was separation-individuation in twin development (Seimon 1980). Psychoanalysts (Burlingham 1952; Leonard 1961) point out that intertwin identification is concurrent with the development of the drive toward separation. While each twin must separate from the mother, the intensity and intimacy of the intertwin bond helps to decrease the pairs' feeling of separateness and independence. Clinicians suggest, in general, that early separation of twins in elementary school as well as through separate friendships is helpful in decreasing intertwin identification.

The question of how this early separation is carried out between mother and twin and between twins has not been described in normally developing twins. Therefore, participants were asked if and when they were separated in school, if they had separate friends, and if they dressed alike. These questions were thought to be most symbolic of the issue of separation-individuation in early childhood.

Language development has been the focus of twin research since the early 1930s. Researchers have suggested that twins have patterns of language acquisition different from single children (Koch 1966; Malstrom 1980). However, researchers disagree on the cause of special language problems in twins. Some researchers attribute their cause to genetic endowments (Mittler 1971); others attribute their cause to environment (Lytton 1980); and others attribute their cause to the interaction between the twins (Leonard 1961). In light of these findings, a question was directed toward language development: "Did you [twins] have any special languages or special systems of communication that excluded your parents?"

Issues of growing up as a twin have been neglected in the twin research. The questions that were posed about adolescence and young adulthood were based on research in child development and twin development. The issue of competition within the twinship was explored: "How did you [twins] handle competition?" "Did you [twins] have the same interests and careers, or did you choose different interests and careers?"

The questions that seemed basic to the nature of the twinship, a close and most intimate relationship to begin with, are: "Do you as a twin relate to others more or less effectively?" "Do skills in relating to one's twin transfer to other relationships, or are other relationships disappointing?"

The development of later physical and psychological separations was covered as well as the progression of the twin bond by asking: "Did you grow further apart as you grew older, or did you remain as close as when you were young children?"

Finallly, twins were asked to put in their own words a definition of what other researchers have termed the *twinning bond*. At the same time they were also asked if they remembered having a unit or a complimentary we-self identity.

ANALYSIS OF THE DATA The interviews were reviewed by both researchers in relationship to the the questions asked and the ensuing responses. The methodology of the study did not include a set of hypotheses about what might be discovered about twinship and its significance for individual development. The conclusions that follow in the ensuing chapters are all the more interesting since they evolved directly from the material of these interviews.

4

PATTERNS OF TWINSHIP

Identity and the capacity to relate closely to others, intimacy, are the focus of the study. Analysis of the data is based on identity formation in the twin subjects. These data suggested different qualities of individuation and different relationships between the twin pairs. One style of individuation was not present for all of the twinships. There were clear patterns that differentiated types of identity, the degrees of separation-individuation, and the relationship formation among the twins who were interviewed.

From these interviews, patterns of twinship emerged naturally. Whereas some twins were able to separate psychologically quite effectively, some twins had great difficulty with psychological separations. The degree to which twins were capable of separation and individual development became the continuum for establishing these patterns of twinship. It became clear that there are dominant patterns of twinship. Indeed, it is possible to group this adult twin population into six types of twinship experiences: (1) unit identity, (2) interdependent identity, (3) split identity, (4) idealized identity, (5) competitive identity, and (6) sibling attachment identity. While some of the twins fit into more than one type of twinship experience, it was relatively easy to determine the pattern that most clearly characterized each twinship—from that of shared identity to individuation. Furthermore, the patterns that began in infancy endured throughout the lives of the twins interviewed.

UNIT   Twins who have merged aspects of
IDENTITY   their personalities have a unit
identity. In other words, there are times when their egos
function as one. There are two manifestations of unit identity:
each twin is half of a whole personality, or both twins need to
do everything the same way. Unit identity is very common in
young twins from birth to 5 years and may manifest itself in
language patterns in which a twin refers to himself/herself as
"we" instead of "I." At times unit identity is also apparent in
the need to dress alike or to be given the same foods and
material objects. Polarization of the twinship with one twin
being the impulsive one and the other being the very control-
led twin is an illustration of the way in which each twin is only
half of a whole personality, which is another aspect of unit
identity.

Manifestations of unit identity, while they are visible and
apparent, are based on an unconscious linking of the egos of
the twin pair. Unit identity fades away with appropriate
parenting, social experiences, and educational exposure.
However, in those instances where the life experiences of the
twins have been deficient in many of these areas, unit identity
will continue to be an important pattern of their twinship.
This pattern is the least adaptive to the growth of individuality and to the development of other significant relationships.
As such, this pattern will complicate the lives of twins and
foster greater reliance upon one another.

Of the 20 sets of identical twins interviewed, unit identity,
as a type of twinning bond, was manifested in three sets of
identical twins. These three sets—identified as having unit
identities—had at the same time their own successful areas of
development, including careers, friendships, and children.
However, they remained psychologically a unit.

These instances of unit identity had certain striking
features in common. Such twins had experienced, in early
childhood, a loss of a constant mothering figure and had been
traumatized by certain social forces. In these instances the
bond between the twins replaced the mother-child bond. The
twins parented each other.

A clear and dramatic picture of this type of twinship was
seen in female identical twins who were victims of the

holocaust. There was no mother from an early age, and the father was absent psychologically. They were raised in a strange new country where they were isolated from the broad native culture and where the language was different from their native tongue.

These twins kept each other alive psychologically and often physically. Their only positive sense of self as children was derived from their presence as twins. Their childhood and adolescence continued to be times of severe emotional and physical abuse. Their bond with one another kept them alive. Today they are women who have achieved much independently in their careers and families, but their view of themselves is that they belong together and will die together.

These twins independently chose physical separation in late adolescence. After this initial separation the more dependent and emotional twin experienced substantial psychological problems. At this period in their lives, they report sympathetically shared experiences of physical pain when one underwent surgery.

Each went on to form very different life-styles and marriages. However, they state that "other people get excluded by their relationship." Presently they have both had two unsuccessful marriages. One of their husbands felt strongly that he could not compete with his wife's sister for affection or involvement.

The regressive pull toward one another has been a major force throughout their lives, but each twin has had other important interpersonal relationships. Nevertheless, one twin said of the other "I knew I would be better off with my sister than with anyone else."

INTERDEPENDENT Twins whose identities are inter-
IDENTITY dependent have always been "best buddies" or the most trusted of friends. The nature of the relationship that interdependent twins have is one in which the twins look to each other for all types of support and assistance. Their lives are interwoven in such a fashion that they may live very close to each other and/or are in communication with each other daily. Although they may

have separate personal and professional lives, they choose to call upon each other as their primary source of emotional support. Such twins state quite clearly that the closest relationship in their lives has been with their twin.

These twins may see each other as quite different or distinctive, but in ways that are usually rather superficial. For example, one twin may describe the other twin as more dominant and gregarious, while the other member of the pair will describe himself/herself as exactly the opposite of the other twin's perception. At any rate these highly interdependent twins have a hard time seeing and describing differences between themselves. If they seek out relationships with others, it is usually a re-creation of the original twinship.

This type of twinning bond has developed from what could be described as very limited amounts of parenting. These twins experienced themselves as a unitary force against their parents, especially against their mother. Among the interdependent twins, there were both fraternal (one set) and identical twins (two sets).

The salient quality of these twins is that their twin relationship is as important or even more important than their relationship to parents. One set of interdependent identical twins was able to say that their mother was overwhelmed and even resented having twins. They could see that she was a more comfortable mother with their younger sibling. In this situation the mother allowed the youngest sibling to act out the mother's aggressions toward the twins. For example, this younger sister was permitted to borrow and to occasionally destroy the twin sisters' clothing without any punishments handed out by their mother.

These sisters each report an excessive closeness and shared identity until the age of 9 when one sister became aware, with the encouragement of a teacher, that she was an individual with her own abilities. This is the sister who later chose to attend college.

Both sisters suffered from anxiety about making new friends and also found it hard to participate in new situations. As young children they avoided other children, and when they had friends they were shared friends. Even into adulthood the types of friendships that are sought out by these twins as most meaningful are those relationships that are twinlike in their intensity.

As one might suspect, these types of twins manifest no ambivalence toward each other. They like each other a great deal. Their families get along and socialize frequently. This type of relationship is oftentimes too gratifying for twins. It hinders their ability to cope or feel safe in the world alone. They can be uncomfortable with the degree of regression their frequent contacts require, but usually not so uncomfortable as to want to change the situation.

SPLIT IDENTITY   Twins whose identity is primarily defined by opposite self-images are described as twins with a split identity. In these situations each twin is consciously and unconsciously assigned a defined role by the parents. One twin is the "good twin"; the other is the "bad" twin. One twin is the competent sibling; the other is the incompetent sibling. One twin is the pretty one, with the sibling being the unattractive one. Further oppositional qualities could be described, and in fact exist.

This type of twin relationship is unbalanced and unequal. One of the twins is idealized by the other as well as by the family, while the remaining twin becomes the scapegoat. This splitting is maladaptive for both twins. The idealized twin takes on narcissistic personality characteristics (i.e., he/she is overinvolved with himself/herself). The devalued twin has a very poor self-concept and very poor self-esteem. He/she will need to struggle toward redefinition later in life in an attempt to develop a more positive identity.

The relationship between twins with split identity is filled with conflict and discomfort, even though they may feel bonded to one another. If there is a resolution of this relationship, it is fraught with difficulties, as trust between the twins has been distorted and abused. As adults, these twins have a hard time establishing relationships with other people that do not reflect their early twin relationships. The good twin appears to be more narcissistic in relation to others, while the twin who grew up with a poor self-concept may feel that it is hard to reach out and develop attachments that are built on equality.

Clearly, the split between twins with this polarized relationship begins early in their lives. In most cases the parents are older and overwhelmed by the pressence of the twin births both emotionally and financially. Since three sets of identical twins and three sets of fraternal twins manifested this type of twinning bond, it became even harder to determine which came first, the mother's blatant favoritism of one twin or the "good" twin's compatability within the family. However, no matter what the etiology of the relationship, the mother makes minute psychological distinctions between her twins, whether real or merely projections of her own psyche.

The mother who psychologically splits her twins into "good" and "bad" has a poorly integrated ego. She may be described as a borderline personality. She is an inadequate mother. It is too difficult for her to relate to her twins as separate individuals—to be ambivalent about both of them. Therefore, she makes one twin the good part of herself and the other twin the bad part of herself. In creating this type of twinship, the mother can control her thoughts, feelings, and responses to her children in an unconflicted manner.

In interviewing twins with this type of mothering, exploration of its origin was pursued. Do you [twins] remember or were you told why one twin was favored over the other? Although participants intellectually and psychologically understood the significance of this question, their responses were based on limited and minute individual differences between the pair. One twin stated, "I was the smiling twin." Perhaps the mother had more positive identification with the unhappy twin or with the least rebellious twin. Obviously, when made by the mother, the distinction was amplified, which evolved into striking differences between the pair.

In all cases these twins reported being conscious of their roles in the family by 5 years of age. One twin reported in kindergarten that she had been assigned the role of being in charge of her sister's mistakes or problems. She cried uncontrollably when she could not stop her sister from spilling paint in her hair. The other twin member was not at all upset or bothered by her own unacceptable behavior. The kindergarten teacher was really confused by the pair.

A fraternal twin set remembers that in first grade one twin was already identified as the depressed and withdrawn twin, while the other was the happy and outgoing twin.

This type of twin relationship, based on inequality and idealization, functions as a unit from early childhood to late adolescence. When separation does occur in late adolescence, life is easier for the "good" twin who has merely lost the bad parts of herself in separation. One twin stated, "I was relieved when we separated." Another stated, "I was liberated when we went to different colleges." Although the "good" twin may suffer through life's problems, the "good" twin is less anxious and less depressed. The "good" twin continues to have an internal image of being special. However, in some instances these twins seem to be incapable of taking full responsibility for themselves and their actions.

Anxiety and depression is suffered by the "bad" twin who has psychologically lost the good parts of herself/himself in the separation. A reintegration of the self is necessary and sought after in different ways for varying symptoms. Usually, these twins have spent many years in psychotherapy or psychoanalysis trying to rework their identity and to feel competent about their own talents. A twin who had spent many years in psychoanalysis felt that she would never have the ability to be bossy and self-centered like her sister. Another highly competent "bad" twin stated that she felt she continued to put herself down by stating that "anybody could do that."

In one situation where the "good" twin and the "bad" twin "shared their dreams," the twin who was treated as the victim was still depressed and anxious, living in the shadow of her sister's approval. A poem that the "approved of" sister felt characterized the relationship illuminates the problems of these twinships.

Success

First they cut a notch across my skins.
My thighs next received a slash ... then belly, chest.
Higher and higher the gouges come.

How long till you get tall enough,
So it'll be my turn to be measured upon you—
no, this is not Procrustes's lullaby.
It's petulance.

Will we always be walls upon which the scars of
successive childhood climbs—must we stand
flat against each other trembling, tiptoe, tense,
while some adult approaches with a knife in their hand?

Bill Knott
Selected Poems (N.Y.: Sun Press, 1977).
Reprinted by permission of the author.

We have been measured against each other, and
measured ourselves against ourselves, and we have
both suffered. We must no longer stand on tiptoe
or slouch down in any proximity to one another.

Anonymous

Obviously, this type of twinning bond is the most conflicted and anxiety provoking for the twin pair. Whereas the incompetent twin hopefully seeks out a more integrated identity upon separation, the narcissistic twin has a difficult time giving up her place as the accomplished twin in the relationship. Adult twins with this type of relationship asked most sincerely, "Why is it so hard to change the relationship?" Clearly, the difficulty in the relationship lies in a basic lack of trust between the twins.

IDEALIZED IDENTITY   Twins who idealize their relationship view the existence of their twinship as the most significant aspect of their life experience. Being born as twins has determined much of their sense of who they are as individuals. These twins feel strongly that there is something special about being twins. They feel committed to their twin relationship beyond any other relationship and place a higher value on their twinship than they do on any other relationship. They think it is "wonderful" to be twins and find it hard to talk about or even to perceive problems in the twinship. Although they may describe fighting or disagreements with one another, they quickly fall into the pattern of sticking together because that is the way they experience their relationship, both consciously and unconsciously.

Such twins truly idealize their relationship, but they often do not find it totally satisfying because it may lack openness and intimacy. Separation and conflict cause a great deal of anxiety for these twins. However, these issues may lead idealized identity twins to be more thoughtful about their identity as independent individuals.

Twins who have an idealized twinning bond have been born into families in which the parents are delighted to have had twins and gain a great deal of narcissistic gratification from the fact that they have twins. The parents of these twins are overly involved in the lives of their twins, and they keep close ties to them through adulthood.

Four sets of identical twins were interviewed who manifested an idealized twinship bond. A symbolic example of this style of twinship can be understood in the words of a twin who stated that twins had "high visibility" and that they could confront the world as a team. These brothers understood that "there was nothing harder than raising twin children." "We were raised as a unit. It was easier." His brother added that "it was more practical to find similar interests for us."

Their mother was not sensitive to their separate interests and feelings, and indeed she encouraged sameness rather than distinctions between the pair. Therefore, these twins had the same friends and the same schooling experiences through college. Because it was easier for the mother, it was easier for these twins to be "inseparable."

In spite of all their close ties and parallel development, these twins do not share thoughts and feelings intimately, nor are they interested in the differences between each other in more-than-a-superficial manner. For example, one twin in making a distinction between himself and his brother, indicated with no emotional overtones, that his brother was the good, warm, sociable one of the pair, while he was the more hardheaded one.

These twins are minimally in touch with their own or other people's feelings and thus leave the impression that they are narcissistic. They have been perceived by their mothers as special because they are twins but not for other attributes. Although they are very successful in their life pursuits, they tend to dominate a relationship outside of their twinship.

COMPETITIVE IDENTITY   Twins whose identities are centered upon competition set standards for each other. These standards are both consciously and unconsciously determined. The intertwin relationship is based upon searching for oneself, desiring everything that the twin sibling has and then reaching beyond for greater achievements. Often competitive twins are highly successful professionals because they show a high degree of pleasure in encouraging the development of each other's talents. At the same time they share a close and caring relationship, demonstrating a great deal of empathy for one another.

The empathic relationship remains as an important feature of their development, while a parallel development of each twin's independent personality is taking place. Competitive twins show a high degree of individual development, clearly defining their ego boundaries and maintaining a close and enduring tie to their twin sibling. They also seek out close and enduring relationships with others.

Parents of competitive twins are comfortable with differences between their twins. They actively encourage differences and allow for competition, while encouraging their twins to maintain closeness. They are supportive of what initially looks like envy on the part of one twin for an achievement of his/her sibling. They are able to allow the envious twin to conquer the new challenge provided by the sibling. In other words they go along with the standards of accomplishments set by their individual twins.

Six sets of identical twins and six sets of fraternal twins manifested competitive twinning bonds. These twins were the most articulate and insightful. They were able to describe similarities and differences within the twinship. Although parents had clearly allowed for distinctions, these twins described times when they felt their identities merged. A mental health professional stated, "As a child I experienced times when boundaries [ego] were drawn around both of us, not between me and him." The psychiatrist felt that merging of egos with his twin led to the capacity to tolerate a lack of ego boundaries, an ability to empathize with others, and an ability to understand reality vicariously.

An identical twin psychologist subject stated that the central issue of twinship was focused on competition. Her summation was that the twinship presented her with an unresolvable dilemma. It was not good to be the same as her sister. Winning in a competition led to guilt over not sharing. Losing also felt bad.

Another identical twin psychologist subject felt that the constant competition with her sister served to assure her that she could do well. But she also felt that if her sister could do it, she could, too, which added a different dimension to the competition.

Competitive twins are the most successful through schooling and later in their life's goals because of the standards they set for each other. One twin told us that she was a high-school valedictorian and her sister was salutatorian. Other competitive twins were first in their class and both received first prize.

Interestingly enough, many of these competitive twins reported having spent time considering issues of their twinship while in some form of psychotherapy. Because of their need for introspection, these twins have a well-developed capacity to empathize with their twins and to relate to others. Often they pursue careers as mental health professionals or artists.

Territoriality, i.e., who is who and what belongs to whom, remains an issue in adulthood. Among this group were found those twins who were geographically distant from each other. However, closeness, which might be seen as regression in the service of the ego, is also available to these twins. For example, one twin described the closeness of the bond to her twin in retelling a slip of the tongue, that occurred when she went to assist her twin in buying a wedding dress. She told the salesperson, "I am the wife of the bride." Earlier in the interview she had stated that twins are born married.

SIBLING ATTACHMENT IDENTITY   Male/female twins have a relationship that resembles that of close siblings. Each twin experiences the other as he/she might a nontwin sibling. Interestingly enough, these twins remember themselves as twins from pictures, stories, and memory. They describe their childhood as containing closely knit experiences. Often they went to the same schools through college. However, the early distinction that they are of different sexes allows them to develop very separate identities.

In the nine sets of male/female twins that were interviewed, there were varying degrees of closeness. Some of these twins actually felt alienated from one another owing to life-style conflicts. Others wished for more closeness in the relationship. Two sets displayed a close and compassionate relationship with one another.

Male/female twins, although sometimes close, display none of the characteristics of the other twinship patterns. Competition is not as intense, as in the competitive twinship pattern, which was described earlier. Dependency needs are not overdetermined. Twinship is not idealized. Identity is not fragmented between the pair. Shared experiences have led those twins to oftentimes be quite compassionate with one another.

CONCLUSION   In this sample, these six discrete patterns of twinship experiences represent a continuum of psychological closeness and interaction. These patterns range from an all-pervasive closeness, which includes a merging of identities, to close attachments and caring feelings that allow for individuality to develop. Whereas, all of our twin subjects shared a bond of twinship, the characteristics of the nature of these bonds varied from twin pair to twin pair. A thread that ran through the fabric of twinship experiences is that of caring for each other and being concerned with the other's well-being. Further, it became clear that the relationship twins experience is primary and determined by parenting. The next chapter will explore how parental involvement creates the twinning bond.

5

Parenting and the Development of the Twin Relationship

Of long-standing interest for developmental psychology is the issue of what constitutes adequate parenting. The most recent research in developmental psychology suggests that child rearing is a two-way process. The child has an effect on his/her parents, and the parents respond to the child's behavior. Interaction determines the nature of parent-child bonding (Ainsworth 1974; Bell 1977; Bowlby 1958; Chess and Thomas 1963; Lytton 1980). Other researchers have demonstrated the necessity of mothering for the survival of the child (Bower 1976). Psychoanalytic theory describes the process involved in adequate mothering from a clinical perspective (Bernstein and Warner 1981).

If all the evidence from theory and research undeniably indicates that the child affects his/her parents and, in turn, that the parents affect their child, what must be the impact of twin children on parenting? And conversely, what is the impact of parenting on twins?

From the material contained in these interviews, it became clear that the most significant determinant of the relationship between twins is the nature of their interaction with their parents. In other words there is no unitary type of relationship between twins. The twin relationship is a reflection of parental attitudes and interactions. Within this sample there were notable differences in parental styles that helped to create the distinct patterns of twinship that have been observed. This chapter will describe these distinctive parental styles that led to the patterns of twinship described in the previous chapter. That is, the parental effect on the twinship will be described, and the twins' effect on parents will be addressed.

UNIT
IDENTITY
For those twins whose identity is shared in such a way that they have a unit identity, parenting was extremely limited, and at the least, it was psychologically abusive. These twins exhibit a relationship that is reminiscent of the relationships among children raised in wartime concentration camps (Bowlby 1958). Just as the unfortunate children of World War II turned to each other as one might to a parent, these twins turned to each other. From each other, they received physical comfort, a degree of psychological security, and a constant trustworthy presence. Their lack of parenting created an extreme dependency—indeed, a traumatically caused symbiotic tie.

Among the twins interviewed was a pair who had experienced, during the early years of their lives, the wartime loss of their mother and the confusion and chaos of a concentration camp existence. Although one of these twins remembers the bombings and the troops marching into her home, she has no memories of her mother. Furthermore, any recollection of her father and stepmother are bleak at best. "Our closeness was enforced. . . . we knew that it was always better to be together."

For these twins their enforced unity of experience continued until they left home in adolescence. They maintained their own close survival through these years, which is reflected in the fact that they slept together until one left home.

Another set of twins, who grew up with a series of maids and who have few recollections of their early relationship with their mother, described their bond as "us" against "them." While the actual circumstances of their lives were different from the twins described earlier, they, too, were in desperate need of each other's psychological support.

They each report that even at 10 years of age their father could not tell them apart. Their relationship with their mother was so distant that they remember as children that she could not understand what they were saying—although they report not having any special language. In adolescence the loss of their father and their mother's inability to share her feelings with them increased their dependency upon one another.

Seeing each other as their necessary "superego" (i.e., parental authority) characterized the upbringing of another set of identical twins with a unit identity. These twins, although raised in an intact middle-class family, experienced their parents as very busy and unaffectionate. They half-jokingly said that their parents had distinguished between them by giving them different names.

Within this pair, "us" against "them" was the pattern of relating. They were their own parents. These twins report that during their adolescence they did not speak with their father for months at a time. When they decided to go away to college, they took care of each other in a parental fashion.

Presently, each talks about the nature of the twinship as one in which ego boundaries are loosely defined. For example, in their unsuccessful marriages, they had unrealistic expectations of their partners. They found it difficult to understand where their spouses' psyches stopped and where their own psyches began. They seem to have difficulties with relationships and expressed wishes to merge with other people, since this was their accustomed mode of relating to each other.

Deprivation of maternal relationships among the twins with unit identity in this study was of paramount significance for their intertwin relationship. Given the early childhood experience in which trust was extremely limited, these twins had to rely upon each other. Nevertheless, they do not appear to have developed unconditional trust in each other. For example, these adults recall experiences when they had to confront the real world individually. By and large, as individuals they could cope for an extended time with their careers and families without turning to each other for support.

Among these three sets of twins, each pair indicated that they directed themselves individually in opposite directions.

For example, one twin was the controlling twin and the other was the twin in need of help. In the second set, one twin was labeled the bully and the other was the more compliant. In the third set, one twin was practical and business-oriented, while the other was the homemaker.

These twins illustrate the self-creation of differences, which Farber (1981) suggested in her reanalysis of the early data of identical twins reared apart. It may be that twins with a unit identity must make these distinctions between themselves in an attempt to secure their own separateness and mental health. Furthermore, they appear freer to be critical of each other and to be physically separated than do the interdependently bonded twins. Their relationship contains degrees of ambivalence about one another. They do not idealize each other, but they still maintain a unit identity.

The common characteristic of unit identity twins is the lack of a significant other relationship outside of the twinship. Such twins become each other's parents and constant emotional supports. They may separate and live in different locations, but the twin is their most important other. When other relationships get too hard for them, they return to their twinship as the primary source of their strength.

INTERDEPENDENT IDENTITY Whereas twins with a unit identity make very little mention of their parents, interdependent twins state clearly that their twin is more important than their mother or father. However, their limited parenting is not due to any traumatic event in their lives or any extremely hostile environment; rather it is a function of their parents' inability to interact with their twins in any kind of positive fashion. Some of these interdependent twins expressed the feeling that their mothers in particular felt excluded from the twin relationship.

Overall, these parents were not happy to have twins, finding it to be an economically and psychologically challenging experience. For those twins whose parents are not psychologically equipped to parent them, the twin relationship holds more gratification, pleasure, and shared experiences than the relationship with their parents. Furthermore, one is struck by the unambivalent and clearly positive feelings these twins have for one another, which is not found in any other pattern of twinship.

Twin sisters who are both teachers and who live within 3 miles of each other are examples of this type of bond. Born into a family that was hoping for a boy, the father was disappointed with his twins. The mother felt guilty that she had not had a boy. Although the mother was present physically, she was not psychologically in tune with her twins. She labeled her twins in a "them" and "us" fashion. The parents expected these girls to be the same and to share thoughts, feeling, and possession. As a result interdependent twins accept that they will participate with each other in most aspects of their lives.

The twin teachers mentioned earlier shared mothering responsibilities among all of their combined families' children. They enjoyed being together because there was no need to communicate, as there was with other friends and even their husbands. They assumed that each had the same thoughts and feelings. It was not necessary to express them overtly all of the time. They are aware that children and husbands are of secondary importance to the primary place held by their twin.

Fraternal twin sisters also manifest an interdependent bond. One twin recalls that her parents were the "up and coming professionals." Their birth was both financially and psychologically overwhelming. Although the mother nursed both of them, it was emotionally difficult for her to deal with both of them. She went back to work, with the household help left with the care of the twins.

One twin cannot remember her parents making any distinctions between them. Often they were both called by the common syllable of their rhyming names. They were both "bright and above average" in their parents' perceptions. They were encouraged to be together, to dress alike, and to share everything, even boyfriends, until they went to separate colleges. These twins determined, in advance of applying to colleges, that they would stand a better chance of acceptance as scholarship students if they applied to different colleges. Their separation, as they explained it, was based on reality considerations.

Even when separated these twins talked to each other almost every day. At one point in their lives, the twin with the more stable life-style took over for her sister as the mother of her sister's child because her sister could not handle the responsibility.

Although these twins have very different careers, their lives are intertwined. They count on each other like a child might depend on a parent. Unfortunately, their mother still gives them the same Christmas presents.

A common characteristic of this identity pattern is that the quality of the relationship between parents and twins is very inadequate. The mother gives up her control and significance for the relationship between the twins. She permits her twins to rely increasingly upon each other. It would appear that these parents assume there is a special potency to "twoness" and overtly or indirectly support the twins' shared experiences.

Shared experiences become ideal experiences for these twins, who then do not have a need to actively seek out other relationships. They do the same things at the same time. They get married to people that both of them can enjoy and choose careers that both can relate to. They continue to be close to one another through all of their life experiences. As their parents have not made distinctions between them, it appears that these twins create differences between themselves (Farber 1981), which are tolerable in the face of such closeness.

SPLIT IDENTITY   Both identical and fraternal twins manifested a split identity. These twins have experienced positive parenting for being twins. The mother and father are usually very excited about having twins because of the special attention that twins attract. One twin reported that her father continually took 16 mm movies of them as they were growing up. The mother's greatest joy was having them dressed beautifully alike. However, the mother is unable to relate to each child as a distinct human being. She relies heavily on her fantasies and projections, making one twin into the positive aspect of herself and the other twin into the negative aspect of herself. In doing this the mother does not have to deal with her ambivalence about child rearing, in general, or her children, specifically.

Obviously, a mother who must do this is not a psychologically healthy person. Most likely she would have a hard time dealing with one child at a time, but two is too much for her to handle. Her enjoyment in raising twins is the narcissistic pleasure she gets from others. "Oh, aren't they cute!" is what is important to this type of mother. Oppositional labels—good/bad, happy/sad, star/victim—help the mother relate to her children in an unconflicted manner throughout childhood and as long as the twins themselves respond to their label.

This of course does nothing positive for the twins' growth and development. In the family they function as a unit, which extends to their schooling and friendship experiences. They are dressed alike and kept together as long as possible. Even though the mother perceives her twins differently, she expects them to be exactly alike for all appearances and remembrances. Therefore, she stresses closeness and sameness—a strong interidentification..

In this situation where together the twins make a unit, with one twin representing the positive aspect of their identity and the other twin representing the negative aspect of their identity, the interdependence between the twins becomes conflicted. The "good" twin gets tired of taking care of her "bad" sister, and the "bad" sister gets tired of being measured as less than her sister. These twins split up in adolescence and seek out more gratifying relationships that are based in reality.

Although these twins may still love each other, they do not love being twins, split copies of one another—halves of a whole. These are the twins who see twinship as "freaky." The mother has no insight into her children's needs for independence or their feelings of resentment toward one another. She continues to treat them differently but to act like they are clones of one another.

One twin stated, "After 3 years of psychoanalysis, when I was 30 years old, I realized that my mother and I had a different relationship than my mother and my sister. When I realized that she just talked about us as being the same but treated us differently, it was easier to relate to her. I started to give up trying to please her all the time because, of course, I couldn't please her—only my sister could please her."

Obviously, understanding and accepting the complexity of the relationship between mother and twins who have been split is quite difficult for these twins to internalize. The mother is never capable of accepting what she has perpetrated and longs, unrealistically, for her twins to be close. The idealized twin wants to keep her prized place. Thus, the devalued twin is left with the real job of separating from the family and feeling good about herself, which is quite a difficult venture.

The ability of the devalued twin to reintegrate her sense of self varied. Different degrees of resolution of the inequality of the twinship were apparent: there was a seriously depressed and anxious twin who still looked to her sister for approval; another who felt alienated from her family, while her sister allowed her parasitical existence to continue; pairs who denied what had happened and longed for closeness between them; a pair who were still fighting it out; and a pair who seemed very distant from each other.

The common characteristic of this bond is mistrust. The mother—and the family as a whole—has divided the twins while at the same time expecting them to appear to be the same. The mother's creation of this tumultuous bond of closeness, merger, and distrust is a difficult one to resolve for all involved.

IDEALIZED TWINS   The idealized twins in this sample were all identical twins. All of these twins were born into families who had looked forward to their twin births and who enjoyed the fact that their children were twins. One twin stated, "My mother had just lost a child, so when we were born she felt we were a special gift."

These parents try to treat their children according to the philosophy of "even Steven." If one twin gets something, so does the other. An extreme example are parents who built an extra room on their house when their twins said they wanted their own rooms. Further, these types of parents felt that their children needed to do everything the same and to have everything the same. If one twin had problems in something, a tutor was brought in to keep them neck and neck.

Reflecting on his parenting, one twin recalls, "We were never encouraged to have separate identities, but we weren't discouraged either." His brother added that their parents indoctrinated them into being twins. Although these twins report physically fighting with each other, they enjoyed being twins, being like each other. They both thought that "getting attention as a unit was a plus." They feel that their extra visibility was what they needed to make it socially. They maintain fond memories of being twins, and they would choose to be twins again. They state "getting attention as a unit was a plus."

In most cases these twins have stayed in close contact with their parents and each other. Periods of separateness have been tolerable and meaningful for them. As their parents have not valued their thoughts and feelings as much as they have paid attention to their being twins, these twins usually find other relationships personally satisfying.

Characteristic of this group of twins is their good feelings about being twins and their long-shared relationship that is not especially conflicted or especially intimate. In fact these twins have a hard time really talking to each other about their differences—their life-styles. In this way the twinship maintains itself as a positive childhood memory.

COMPETITIVE TWINS

Both identical and fraternal competitive twins clearly recall that their parents made distinctions between them. Although they may have some ambivalence about their parents, they feel that their parenting was adequate. They are able to articulate similarities and differences within their twinships. They also remember that they received a great deal of attention for being twins from their families and friends.

A clear example of good mothering was described by identical twins who were thought to be fraternal and raised as fraternal twins. They were told that they were no more similar than any two sisters. They indicate that their parents were deliriously happy to have twins and took on the task of raising them "intelligently and psychologically." These girls were never dressed alike and were in separate classrooms. They had separate friends, and separate interests were encouraged.

Their mother, who encouraged them to master the twinship, had them practice being separated before they went to college. They went away to separate summer camps, and they wrote to each other and sent each other taped messages. When they did separate and go to college, they each took on very different life-styles. Only within the last 5 years have they lived relatively close to one another. They find the closeness comforting but also threatening to their individuality. They suggest that the problem of raising twins as individuals is quite difficult even when there is more-than-adequate sensitivity on the part of the mother.

A set of fraternal twins humorously indicates that their parents operated under a very wise doctrine of "separate but equal." They were seen as clearly distinct individuals, not as "two peas in a pod." They were never referred to as twins. Neither was favored. Each received the praise or the blame that was appropriate. Although their parents attempted to separate them, they spent a good deal of time together because they were both in advanced-placement classes. The competition, which was fierce between them, was encouraged by their parents. They were also encouraged to have separate friends. Their separation from one another was gradual, as the parents took into account the closeness of their relationship.

However, not all competitive twins had parents who were psychologically sophisticated. Some competitive twins were somewhat of a hardship to their families financially but were also accepted with great joy. These parents clearly made distinctions between their children. They were treated as individuals with neither twin being favored. In all of these cases, the families had high expectations of their twins for achievement. The family goals and values were clearly delineated. Working within the family standards, the twins competed with one another for parental praise and attention. Thus, competition and achievement were encouraged by the parents. Although these twins were not necessarily separated in school and separate interests were not encouraged, the twins managed to develop their own interests and their own styles of relating to others.

To a certain degree these twins also report that they measure their accomplishments against each other's standards. One twin stated, "I knew if she could do it, so could I." Her own inference followed that the nature of competition was changed by the knowledge that she was an able competitor.

Parents of twins with competitive identity were able to deal with their children fairly and on an individual basis. Although they may have realized the problems inherent in raising twins, they did not give into parenting them as "a duo." They consciously tried to give each twin what he or she may have needed. They allowed for the complications of closeness, competition, and intimacy. These twins developed into highly productive and empathic individuals.

This pattern of twinship was most representative of the entire sample; 8 sets of fraternal twins and 9 sets of identical twins made up the 17 sets in this category. All of these twins vividly remember that their parents encouraged competition between them, and this experience served them in a positive way in their own development. As adults these twins expressed various degrees of comfort with their competitive styles of relating to the world as well as with their adult twin siblings.

SIBLING ATTACHMENT IDENTITY In male/female twins, gender differentiation made it much esier for their parents to relate affectively to each twin. Although competition was stressed in these families, identity between the twins was never confused. The male twins had a different role in the family, different toys, different friends, and even different ambitions compared with their twin sisters. Parental affection and family values affected their adult closeness. Close families in which many significant experiences were shared led to lasting bonds of affection and compassion for each other.

IMPLICATIONS FOR PARENTING Given the material from these interviews, which is clinical and retrospective, we can extrapolate the nature of positive parenting of twins. Primarily, the parents must be aware that their influence on the development of individuality in their twins is crucial because parents create the nature of the twinning bond, which endures throughout the lives of their twins.

Parents of twins need to develop separate, individual, and equivalent styles of relating to their children. Inadequate parenting, which does not develop individuality between twins, creates a highly interdependent relationship for twins, which is difficult, if not impossible, to transcend. Favoritism by parents—i.e., the "good" twin and the "bad" twin—creates an enormous amount of conflict and ambivalence for twins, while also giving both twins an unrealistic perception of their own abilities. Idealization of the twinship by parents fosters a need for remaining identified as a twin that does not necessarily fit into the later life-styles of these twins.

Clearly, parents who can distinguish between their twins and allow for competition and closeness are the most effective. Parents who have long-term goals for rearing twins as individuals will help create a relationship between them that will be one that they will value and use for comfort, support, and encouragement for the rest of their lives.

IMPLICATIONS FOR THERAPY Clinical case studies have suggested that the bond between twins is a unitary force that produces conflict, anxiety, ambivalence, and problems with separation-individuation. This study indicated that the bond between twins may be a life-sustaining force in some situations. In other situations the bond may create a comfortable but limiting interdependence, or the bond may be conflicted and ultimately insignificant. Idealization of the bond leads to an empty relationship between twins. Competition between them is healthy and productive. Gender differences are more crucial than intertwin identification for male/female twins.

The therapist who understands the nature and significance of the intertwin relationship for the twin patient will have greater insight into the problems confronting the patient.

6

THE SIGNIFICANCE OF SEPARATION

Identical twins who have been separated at birth have been the focus of research on genetic determinants of identity since the first twin studies at the turn of the century (Mittler 1971). Recent research at the University of Minnesota by Bouchard indicates that there are striking similarities between identical twins reared apart on all aspects of functioning (Holden 1980). Such research amplifies the question, how does separation affect twins? What does separation mean to identical twins?

Bouchard's research highlights the significance of the genetic blueprint on all aspects of human development. This research, although as yet incomplete, has been widely covered by the media in order to locate potential subjects, as well as to present his tentative findings. As scientists we question whether Bouchard is randomly selecting his sample by advertising for his subjects. Thus, criticism of the research design and the findings may be in order. Further, the research can be criticized for perpetuating the cultural myth that twins are copies of one another, that twins are merely "two peas in a pod."

Bouchard's research appears to be a replication of the earlier research on identical twins reared apart, which Farber (1981) has reanalyzed. Farber's argument that intrapsychic conflict between twins creates differences between them is provocative and insightful. Using the same type of data as Bouchard, Farber comes to an entirely different and enlightening conclusion as to the "real" meaning of separation for twins. Farber suggests that any personal knowledge of twinship will cause psychic conflicts for twins, who then strive for individuality, "artificially," in an attempt to gain their own sense of self. Therefore, it is more likely that twins who have no knowledge of one another will develop very similarly. Further, Farber's argument indicates that separation has a different meaning when looked at from an intrapsychic perspective rather than from a genetic point of view.

Psychoanalytically-oriented clinicians have seen separation-individuation as the key issue in twin development. Engel (1975) writes:

> A central developmental issue for twins concerns the fact that separation-individuation must ultimately involve the twins as well as the mother. Indeed there is an indication that the intimacy and intensity of the interaction between twins may accelerate the separation from the mother only to be replaced by a prolonged symbiosis between the twins whose separation and individuation from each other may be consequently delayed. (p. 32)

Along the same line of reasoning, Seimon (1980) states:

> While societal myths popularized the notion that twins are happy in their twinship, in reality there is a great deal of ambivalence. Characteristic psychological disturbances occur when twins who function as a unit separate in adulthood. . . . The resolution of the fusion between self and twin can become a compelling influence in adult development and a crucial determinant in the formation of other intimate relationships. (p. 387-88)

Once again the experiences of clinicians with twin patients who have developmental disturbances—while they contribute to a general understanding of twin development—do not explain the developmental process of identity formation and the ability to engage in close or intimate relationships.

Within our sample of twins, only a limited number of twins were unable to cope with psychological separation from their twin. These twins were either those with a unit identity or those with interdependent identity. Split identity twins were found to be ambivalent about their relationship and actively sought out separation and individuation from their twin. Idealized twinships present such pairs with a confusion over leaving the image of twinship and its narcissistic gratification; consequently, there is less difficulty with the process of individuation from one's twin. Competitive twins in our sample consciously confronted separation and individuation from their twin. They have been able to evolve from states of conflict about separation to stages of awareness about its significance in their lives. For male/female twins separation-individuation occurs naturally and comfortably.

UNIT IDENTITY Among the group of unit identity twins were twins who had lived apart, even at great distances from one another. There were twins whose lives were different but who had not succeeded in functioning emotionally on their own. The fact of their psychological need for each other led to an inability to separate later in life.

A female identical twin stated that she always took care of her sister in moments of distress. Presently, the twin sister's life was upset by divorce, problems with her children, and financial difficulties. At this juncture the sisters decided to live together again. They could talk to each other, jointly raise the children, and pool their finances. Further, their interdependency went beyond these realities. It appeared that their lives together were more balanced than when they were apart. The more controlling and emotionally contained twin functioned in place of certain aspects of her sister's ego. The twin in need of emotional support functioned more effectively with the help of her sister's ego strength. The reciprocal nature of the relationship was accepted by both.

Male identical twins who separated after graduation from college to pursue different careers tried to develop successful relationships with women. They married and had children, but neither marriage was successful. Presently, the brothers, who now live in the same community, spend time together with all of their children. One of these twins admitted that for almost 20 years their relationship had not been close—they lived in different cities while pursuing different careers. In adversity they were back together once again. They shared and pooled their resources to care for their children.

These twins were geographically separated for a long time and made an effort to separate psychologically. For example, they mentioned being angry with each other for a period during their geographical separation. However, they were not able to move into other meaningful relationships. Although they were aware of "self-consciousness" about their twinship, they indicated that their bond was "inevitable."

The illustrations given indicate that these types of twins are not able to separate psychologically from each other. Aspects of their egos remain merged. Because these twins have had a hard time separating, they have had a difficult time understanding other people's ego boundaries. Their problem marriages are evidence that certain expectations they had of their wives were not possible to fulfill.

INTERDEPENDENT IDENTITY Whereas unit identity twins demonstrate some conflict and ambivalence over their twinship and attempt to separate from one another, interdependent twins are seemingly unambivalent about their relationship and therefore do not find it necessary to separate psychologically. Separation-individuation from each other is not as important as the shared relationship between the twins. Obviously, they are separate human beings, but the bond of attachment and the need for each other exist as part of their development.

Furthermore, there is so much positive gain from being twins that twinship is valued over individuality. As these twins choose to relate to each other in this very close way, they seem to have chosen a symbiotic relationship. Our feeling is that this type of relationship has many more positive and healthy shared experiences than do most symbiotic ties.

For example, these twins enjoy phoning each other and just chatting or giving mutual advice and help on a daily basis.

They take care of each other's children, and their families socialize together. They are truly each other's friend. They appear to enjoy their mutual dependency with its predictability and security. They appreciate each other and accept each other for who they are, not for what the other is accomplishing.

The picture that emerges about these interdependent twins regarding psychological separation is one in which the elements of satisfaction with their relationship are more significant than any effort to strive for greater achievements as individuals. Whether they will achieve separation from each other is highly questionable.

These twins seem to fit Engel's (1975) description of twins who separate from the mother earlier than single children but who are unable to achieve psychological separation from each other.

SPLIT IDENTITY Separation-individuation is imperative for the psychological well-being of the devalued member of the twin pair. In all cases this was the most fundamental issue in their development. Within the sample those twins who were labeled the "bad twin" by the family and who had not been able to separate psychologically from the family, their twin, and their label manifested notable degrees of clinical depression and anxiety.

Within the entire sample of 40 sets of twins, only two individuals, who were part of the split identity pattern, had histories that included self-destructive tendencies. One of these "bad twins" had made a suicide attempt as an adolescent and remained markedly depressed and withdrawn as an adult. Another "bad twin" had a series of serious accidents that she labeled as possibly self-destructive. She appeared to be anxious and somewhat confused about her relationship with her sister.

Both of these individuals were limited in their abilities to relate to others and to accept their own strengths. One twin stated, "I continually put myself down by saying that anybody could do that." In that way she denied having any special

talents or unique abilities. Because these twins had incorpor-
ated into their view of themselves a sense of themselves as
deficient in comparison with their "good" twin, they
remained unable to function as individuals with positive self-
esteem. Indeed, they continued to feel inadequate in all roles
of their lives, even when it was clear to them that they had
made significant achievements in some spheres.

However, not all of the devalued twins remained locked
into their roles. Most of these twins had sought out therapy as
adolescents or as young adults in an effort to gain a perspective on their roles in the family. Two of these individuals had
had a long analysis that enabled them to overcome their
feelings of inadequacy and helped them to understand their
ambivalence toward their twin and their parents. They both
reported that overcoming their family role was what
eventually made is possible to think of themselves positively
and to function independently.

In all cases the "good" twins found it hard to give up the
twin relationship because of the numerous positive elements
and the narcissistic gain for themselves. They had been
favored, idealized, and set as a role model by the family.
Giving up this position or even having some insight about it
was too painful and guilt inducing. The "good" twins remain
identified as a twin but have little awareness of the problems
confronting their twin brother or sister.

At some point in their adult lives, split identity twins may
come to understand the roles that they were assigned because
of their mothers' unconscious projections. Yet even with such
intellectual comprehension, the "good" twins do not seem to
be able to comprehend the psychic suffering of their twins. On
the other hand, the devalued twins have a hard time making
peace with their childhood introjects.

Separation-individuation for split identity twins who
were involved in this study was, paradoxically, easier for
them to attain. Although these twins were differentiated in a
manner that produced long-term detrimental effects for both
twins, they were indeed differentially responded to by the
mother on the basis of her unconscious projections from an
early point in their development.

IDEALIZED   The separation-individuation process
IDENTITY   in idealized twins is more difficult to
understand and describe than for the other patterns of twinship. Since in essence the sample of twins who are part of an
idealized pattern of twinship each identifies with the concept
of "twinness" rather than with their twin, it is the image of
duality that is idealized. They perceive each other as part of a
team. The team aspect of their identity, being twins, is what is
shared by them.

Among the twins interviewed, separation from this identification (being part of a twin pair) was not attained. There was
an enormous amount of narcissistic gratification gained from
being a twin, which remained as a stable and enduring part of
their identities.

Nevertheless, the intertwin identification has never been
especially intimate. Psychological separation followed since
their emotional relationship was not as intense as was found
in other patterns of twinship.

This pattern of twinship is reflective of a style of family
life that is not commensurate with the expression of feelings.
As such the total family environment does not foster closeness
and communication of meaningful feelings. In other words
these twins have had parallel developmental experiences with
a minimal amount of shared feelings.

This situation leads to a distinctly different pattern of
twinship. Whereas in all the other patterns of twinship the
twins have experienced much mutuality and sharing of
thoughts and feelings, these twins have very little experience
with shared feeling. They have used the twinship to attract
attention socially, but such twins do not go on to understand
other people's thoughts and feelings.

Since these twins have not had a close relationship, separation is not especially difficult for them. In fact these twins
find separation rewarding on a personal level. In general they
do not socialize with one another and have pursued different
life-styles. One married twin with children said that her
unmarried sister did not visit because she found her sister's
family life so different and dull in comparison with her own
life. Neither of these twins missed each other enough to care

to change their priorities. Another set of male twins reported that their wives were very different, implying that they did not like each other's wives nor each other's friends. They did not socialize but would occasionally spend time together alone, which kept their twinship alive.

In conclusion, separation-individuation for these twins is not very conflicted. Although they never separate from the idealization of the twinship, they separate from each other.

COMPETITIVE TWINS As a group the competitive twins have the most potential for growth outside of twinship. This phenomenon is related to their early parent-child interactions, which encouraged individual achievement and progress. Furthermore, that parent-child relationship was one in which the parents were not overly involved in the fact that they had twin children.

Although the mother has tried to make her children independent of one another, there are still problems that are experienced with separation from the twin. It appears that these problems are focused unconsciously on an inability to give up the closeness, comfort, and security of the twinship. Further, as these twins have been trusted friends with shared values and dreams, it is hard for them to find other people who hold them or their ideas as compellingly as did their twin. However, competitive twins are consciously driven to give up their closeness for a wider range of individual rewards. Because these twins have a positive experience with an intimate relationship, they seek out other close relationships and expect to achieve a degree of intimacy.

For our sample of competitive twins, their physical or geographical separation usually took place in adolescence. The separation itself may not have been problematic, but finding other adequate relationships was not always as successful, at least not at first. These twins had amazingly high expectations for their friendships and did not sense that perhaps these expectations were unrealistic. However, competitive twins made a continuing effort to make close emotional attachments to other significant persons in the course of their lives while maintaining the competitive spirit of their twinship.

Separation for competitive twins allowed for a greater range of individual commitment but did not disrupt the psychological tie to one another. These twins reported successful personal lives and careers. Yet at times it was significant for them to return to the immediacy of their twin relationship, which allowed them to be more attuned to new relationships. A twin indicated that being in the same room with her sister was "comforting." She felt very secure with her sister, in a way that was special. This particular twin is a therapist who has dealt with a wide range of people and who has the capacity to form intimate relationships.

In conclusion, what is most striking about this pattern of twinship is the ability of these twins to maintain their own lives as well as their twinship.

SIBLING ATTACHMENT   As there was an apparent lack of intertwin identification in the male/female twins we interviewed, their psychological separation from each other was not as much an issue as it was for the other twinship patterns. Although these twins had shared their childhood and parents, the fact that they were of different genders was for them the crucial distinguishing factor within their family experience. This gender difference meant that they were to a large extent parented differently from each other. In addition their identifications with each other were not more significant than those they had with their other siblings or with their parents.

Consequently, separation from each other was not unduly complicated. These male/female twin pairs separated from each other in late adolescence and followed different careers and personal interests. Reflecting upon their relationship, most of these twins agreed that their twin was special to them. They indicated that they had warm and caring feelings for each other. They seemed to feel that for them twinship had been a positive experience. One twin poetically stated, "I never felt that I didn't get the full birthday party."

In conclusion, the lack of conflict and ambivalence over twinship that these twins experienced in relationship to the other twinship patterns must be attributed to the early sex role differentiation within the family.

DISCUSSION   Clearly, the separation-individuation process for twins is different and more complicated than for single children. From this research it is difficult to determine or even to conceptualize exactly how the first separation-individuation from the mother took place, as we did not explore the earliest experience of separation within the framework of our interviews.

Although psychoanalytic theory predicts a different type of separation from the mother, perhaps an earlier separation, this was not apparent in all of the twinship patterns. Where there was not adequate mothering, this was probably what occurred, with the twin relationship serving as a compensatory relationship in place of the mother-child bond.

Two variations of lack of mothering occurred. In unit identity twins it appeared that the absence of the mother and the trauma of their early childhood experiences served to make them untrusting in general, and even of one another. It is plausible that the stage of basic trust vs. mistrust did not provide adequate consistency and love. This made their lives as well as their twinships fraught with ambivalence and anxiety. However, this bond, which was formed as an interdependency, was impossible to unravel. Psychological separation for these twins was so difficult and unrewarding that they preferred to function within close psychological proximity to each other.

For interdependent twins the presence of the mother and a stable infancy and early childhood allowed these twins to develop basic trust in relationships. These are the twins who most likely separate from the mother earlier than single children but who do not have the ability to separate from each other because of the lack of distinctions that have been made by parental interactions. The interdependency of these twins begins at birth and continues past a point where they should have developed a sense of their own self-worth. In Eriksonian terms the stage of autonomy vs. shame is not resolved successfully, making separation-individuation impossible for these twins to achieve.

Split identity twins have been given definite identities and have separated from the mother in early childhood. The separation from their unit identity as two halves of a whole is dependent on their drive to individuate in adolescence, when environmental influences are significant. From this research it was difficult to discern what factor in development led some devalued twins to seek out therapy to overcome their unhealthy self-images.

As has been stated earlier, separation for idealized twins is not especially conflicted. The separation from leaving the idea of being a twin—the notion of being a team, the emphasis on duality—is what these individuals can not give up in the midst of their individually successful lives. There is an overriding parental gratification that these twins identify with from the state of twinship that continues to be a factor in their own self-images.

Competitive twins separate successfully from one another. Although the process is often painful—indeed they are aware of their ambivalence about being twins—they are able to come to terms with the vicissitudes of their twinship. They take from it the good aspects of their twin relationship. These twins have struggled with psychological separation from each other and seem better able than twins with different developmental patterns to develop satisfying personal lives and careers.

The interidentification between male/female twins is not significant enough to limit their identity formation or their separation from each other.

IMPLICATIONS   In all of the patterns of twinship separation, both physical and psychological, was a critical aspect of separation-individuation. Even for the twins whose lives remained intertwined and interdependent, separations were meaningful, allowing for the development of separate interests and needs. Although separating twins from one another may be difficult from a psychological viewpoint and from a practical standpoint, mental health professionals, parents, teachers, and twins themselves should be made aware of the positive effects of separation. For example, an interdependent twin pointed out that her teacher recognized her academic potential and encouraged her to pursue her talents. This differentiation and encouragement by the teacher allowed this twin to pursue a college education, which her sister did not feel inclined to do. This simple distinction made by the teacher was critical to this woman's self-actualization.

Although we have emphasized the nature of the bond between twins as one that is determined by parenting, we do not mean to indicate that other environmental influences are not significant. Indeed, it appears that all of the influences from society in general that contribute to an image of distinctiveness for twins will be helpful to the development of individuality in twins.

It is our belief that parents, teachers, and mental health professionals should make serious efforts to allow for the development of individuality in twins. Further, we believe that parents and teachers need advice and help in relating to twins as individuals.

7

Nature, Nurture, and Interaction

Twins have been used extensively as subjects of research studies concerning the influence of genetic endowments as compared with environmental influences (Cohen et al. 1977; Gessell 1941; Jensen 1969; Matheny 1980; Mittler 1971; Newman et al. 1937; Shields 1962; Wilson 1978). Psychodynamic research, which also uses twins as subjects, adds a broad dimension to child development research because it considers the psychological interaction between parent and child and the effect of that interaction on intrapsychic growth and development (Burlingham 1952; Dibble and Cohen 1981; Gifford et al. 1966; Leonard 1961; Lytton 1980; Schave 1982; Zazzo 1960).

Child development theorists start with an acceptance of the genetic blueprint. They add to genetic endowments the parent-child relationship and other social forces. Nevertheless, the genetic blueprint is understood as specific, singular, and in a manner of speaking, a limitation upon individual development. The child who is a twin has—in addition to the genetic blueprint—parents, the broader environment and, instantly from the moment of conception, the presence of another. How significant is the presence of an additional primary relationship to the growth of such a child?

We know that parent-child interaction is fundamentally important to the child's development (Bell 1977; Bower 1976; Bowlby 1958; Erikson 1950; Lytton, Conway & Suave 1977;

Mahler 1967; Sullivan 1953). The additional question to raise about twins is, of what importance is this other primary relationship to personality development? The present research is an attempt to begin to look at the effects of twinship on individual development.

THE
INTERACTION
HYPOTHESIS
Farber (1981), after a reanalysis of over 100 case studies of identical twins reared apart, is the only theorist to have suggested that the interaction between twins leads to differences between the pair. Farber speculates that individuality is crucial to the healthy intrapsychic functioning of twins. Thus twins must create "artificial differences" between themselves to attain a sense of individuality.

Niels Juel-Nielsen (1980), who has also conducted research on identical twins reared apart, adds a different dimension to the nature-nurture controversy. He, too, indicates the importance if interaction. Niels Juel-Nielsen writes:

> *The farther one penetrates into the intricacies of the complexity of genetic and environmental factors that together determine the development of individuals, the more one is compelled to admit that there is not one problem but a multiplicity of minor problems—that there is no general solution of the major nor even to any minor problems. (p. 10)*

Looking at nature, nurture, and interaction we reach different conclusions from other twin researchers. Our findings, which differ significantly from the extensive body of twin research, emphasize the significance of interaction between parent and twins as well as interaction between the twins.

We must conclude that when interaction, genetics, and environment are taken together, one can formulate some provocative conclusions about twinship. Generally, identical twins are thought to bear the burden of problems related to twinship. How will they ever separate? How will they ever become individuals? We found that identical twins who have appropriate parenting separate with as much ease or as much difficulty as fraternal twins.

The overriding issue for both identical and fraternal twins is the quality of parenting they have experienced. Within our sample we found well-functioning identical and fraternal twins who had been brought up as individuals. The crucial variable was that the mother interacted with her twins differently, not that they were identical or fraternal twins. The crucial factor was differential interaction between the mother and each of her twins.

Since we did not interview mothers of twins in this study, we cannot be certain whether relating to identical twins as individuals is harder than relating to fraternal twins as individuals. It would seem that greater physical similarities might foster greater similarities in the mother's response to identical twins. However, Burlingham's (1952) point that the mother of identical twins must differentiate between her twins to identify with them and relate to them should be kept in mind. We cannot say how the mothers of our adult identical twins perceived their roles in relation to the identical twins. However, we do know that it was possible for mothers to assist in the development of individuated twins.

Although it appears that it might be easier for the mother of fraternal twins to differentiate between them, this point of view can be challenged on the grounds that fraternal twins are confronting very similar developmental tasks at the same time just as are identical twins. In addition, does the knowledge that her twins are genetically different lead to the mother's greater ease in raising individuals?

Our findings indicate that eight sets of identical twins and seven sets of fraternal twins were raised by mothers who reportedly took their individuality very seriously. Whether a mother is psychologically healthy is fundamental to her capacity to relate to two children at the same time. Therefore, this variable—the mother's psychological well-being—must be considered to be another significant factor in raising twins who are capable of separation and individuation. In conclusion, for these 15 sets of twins, adequate mothering was more important than the genetic givens of their twinship.

**GENETIC
SIMILARITY AS A
DETERMINANT OF
TWO PATTERNS
OF TWINSHIP**
Two patterns of twinship discussed earlier raise even more questions about the significance of genetics and the parental environment. We found that all of the twins with a unit identity and all of the twins with an idealized identity were identical twins.

**Unit
Identity**
Speculating about why identical twins composed the unit identity pattern of twinship, we take into consideration (1) the already understood material about a mother's difficulty in rearing identical twins and (2) the fact that the psychological well-being of mothers of identical twins contributes significantly to whether twins will be experienced by the mothers as individuals or as a unit. All of the mothers of our unit identity twins had, for a variety of reasons, been unable to provide mothering for their children. We do not know whether these same mothers would have been better able to raise a single child, but they were unable to deal with their identical twins.

The situations into which these three sets of unit identity twins were born were ones in which there was chaos and confusion or ones in which there was marked emotional estrangement from the parents, particularly from the mother. One might suspect that these circumstances would have a lasting impact: one in which the child's growth became very disturbed. This did not occur. Unit identity twins are successful in their careers and with their families.

These twins helped each other to achieve positive changes in their environments—changes that altered the early destructive or limited aspects of their realities. In turn the new environments that they actively sought to experience and actively assisted each other to attain served to foster their positive growth and a more healthy and adaptive development.

The combination of genetic factors of identicality and the mother's inability to relate to her children as individuals led to the unit identity pattern of twinship. From the data that we collected, it is not possible to unravel the sequence of significance among genetics, interactions between parents and twins, and interactions between the twins themselves. Was it the mother who could not deal psychologically with identical twins? Did the twins not need the mothering? Was the factor of their identicalness not important at all?

What is most striking about this twinship pattern is that these twins—in spite of very limited mothering, troubled childhoods, and the fact that they are identical twins—were able to develop identities that allowed them to function successfully in the world. They are not psychotic, as might be the expectation for a single child with limited mothering and a very troubled childhood.

Indeed, the interaction between the twins allowed them to separate and individuate. This finding supports Farber's thesis that there is a need for individuality in identical twins. Our conclusion follows that interaction is the most significant determinant of development for unit identity twins.

Idealized Identity

The four sets of identical twins with an idealized identity were well functioning and successful in their personal lives and careers. They, nevertheless, gave the impression that they had limited their spheres of involvement and their horizons both intellectually and interpersonally because they were narcissistically committed to being twins.

Genetic components have clearly played a part in the determination of this twinship because the mother was so involved in the fact that she had given birth to identical twins. However, the interaction between the twins and with the mother seems to be more important than the fact that they were born as identical twins.

The quality of mothering for the idealized identical twins was not as limited or limiting as the mothering of unit identity twins. In fact the mother of the idealized identity twins was overly involved with her children and with their "twinness." The mother's presence and involvement allowed her twins to separate and individuate. The quality of twinness could not be left behind until they reached adulthood and went their separate ways. At that time in their lives, when they separated, they report having experienced great satisfaction and feelings of liveliness in regard to establishing their own relationships as individuals.

Our impression was that the idealization of the twinship was a function of the interaction between the mother and her twins. Although genetic similarities were important in developing idealization of the twinship, the genetic endowment, the fact of identicalness, cannot be considered the determinant of the idealization of the twinship.

ENVIRONMENTAL INFLUENCES ON TWINSHIP PATTERNS

For the remaining patterns of twinship—interdependent identity, split identity, competitive identity, and sibling attachment identity—environmental influences, including parent-child interactions, were more significant than the genetic makeup of these individuals. Both identical and fraternal twins were found in the remaining four patterns of twinship.

Of the three sets of interdependent identity twins, two sets were identical and one set was fraternal. Of the six sets of split identity twins, three were identical and three were fraternal. Among the competitive identity twins, eight were identical and seven were fraternal. And nine sets of fraternal male/female twins manifested a sibling attachment identity.

Monozygosity or dizygosity was established as reported by the twins. An interesting illustration of the importance of the mother's conviction about the zygosity of her twins was reported by a set of split identity sisters. In this case the mother purposely labeled her twins as identical. This woman apparently felt that the fact that two eggs could be fertilized simultaneously meant that she had had sexual relations with two men. Therefore, she consciously insisted that her children were identical twins. The twins were dressed identically but were always conscious of vast differences in their physical appearances and in their personalities. As young adults they realized that they were so different they must indeed be fraternal twins.

A set of identical twins who were born from separate placentas were thought to be, and grew up as, fraternal twins. At the age of 20 when one twin was found to have a rare blood type, the sister's blood type was determined and found to be identical with her sister's. This meant for these competitive identity twins that they had to adjust their views of each other.

Perhaps the lesson to be learned from these two stories is that "reality is in the eye of the beholder." Environment shapes convictions about issues; including genetic issues.

Interdependent Identity Identical and fraternal twins were found within the parameters of the interdependent identity twinship pattern. Thus, zygosity was not the only determinant of this pattern of twinship. Most specifically, interaction between the twins and their mothers resulted in this unique pattern of twinship.

The interdependent, interrelated manner in which these twins function is particularly clear when they are dealing with new experiences. Many of these twins reported uneasiness in new situations. These twins deal with reality best through their interactions—sometimes a telephone call is all that is necessary to enable them to handle some new experience.

We must conclude that the interaction between the twins of this identity pattern is the crucial determinant of its existence. The environment and the genetic blueprint were minimally important in relationship to the interaction between these twins.

Split Identity Similarly, the split identity twin groups were divided equally with three sets of identicals and three sets of fraternals. Once again zygosity was not the significant factor in the determination of this twinship pattern. The mother's interaction with her twins and the ensuing relationship that was formed between the twins resulted in this twinship pattern.

These twins attempt in all ways to create different environments for themselves because they are intensely uncomfortable with each other. They attempt to avoid being compared with each other. There is an estrangement between these twins that is far greater than the genetic endowment or the effects of the environment could ever explain. The mother's initial distinction between her twins is the most significant factor in the formation of split identity patterns of twinship.

Competitive Identity   The eight sets of identical twins and the seven sets of fraternals who composed this twinship pattern also support the importance of environmental influence on the development of identity. Indeed, the interaction within the family structure, with particular reference to the mother's relationship with her twins, is once again the determinant of this twinship pattern.

These twins use their environments to grow and separate from each other. Our impression was that without the environment, e.g., schooling, these twins would have felt psychically trapped by each other. Therefore, they used what was offered by their surroundings and went on to measure themselves against the internal or external standard that one twin set for the other in an effort to feel separate. One twin stated that if he did not compete with his brother, he felt their ego boundaries were less distinct.

Environmental influences bear strongly upon the development of this pattern of twinship. Furthermore, competitive identity twins maximize what is offered by their surroundings and are notably accomplished individuals.

Sibling Attachment Identity   Nine sets of male/female twins were interviewed. Particularly with this twinship pattern, questions about the significance of genetic endowments as compared with environmental influences became more complex. In all cases and emphatically, these male/female twins stated that distinctions between them were based upon sex role differentiation made by the parents. In other words mothers related to each of their twins on the basis of sex rather than on the basis of their twinship. While these twins report a special closeness that does not necessarily exist with their other siblings, they did not appear to have experienced an intertwin identification in the same ways as the other twin groups.

Clearly, the mother in these situations could distinguish between her twins. The mother makes distinctions by utilizing the physical features of her twins as well as by incorporating her understanding of sex role differences in relation to each child. Furthermore, these twins follow somewhat different developmental sequences, which means that distinctions in relationship to the children are facilitated by the givens of their development. More simply stated, boys develop in most areas more slowly than girls, which allows mothers to distinguish between their individual growth patterns.

Sex role distinctions enabled the male/female twins in our sample to be reared as individuals. The contributions of heredity and environment appear to be of at least equal weight for these twins. The more significant result from these interviews is the clarity with which mothers of such twins were able to interact distinctly and differently with each twin.

Once again, in the sibling attachment identity pattern of twinship, the nature of the mother's interaction was as significant as heredity and environment.

TWINS AND THE PSYCHOSOCIAL ENVIRONMENT Twins create responses from their environments that are unique to them. The effect of the environment as a whole upon the development of twins became an increasingly important determinant of development for our twin subjects. Although our purposes did not initially include an exploration of the effect of the broader social environment on twins, twins whom we interviewed indicated that social and cultural stereotypes about twinship inhibited their development as individuals. Indeed, it may have been that they were motivated to participate in these interviews out of a need to make clear to others the development of identity in twins.

In general, most twins who participated in this study felt that the continual attention that was focused on them because of their twinship was difficult to accept. Exceptions were our four sets of idealized identity twins who enjoyed and used the attention focused on their twinship.

The response of society tells us something about the unconscious needs of singletons to have a twin at least in fantasy (Burlingham 1952). The problem area for twins lies between other people's fantasies about having a twin and the reality of their being twins.

Some twins expressed that they oftentimes felt like "freaks" while growing up, a walking sideshow on four legs. In addition some of our subjects felt that people's expectation that they be similar and emotionally close was confusing for them as individuals. In many respects these twins had to defend against the outside world's expectation that they would share a unit identity. For most twins in our sample, this was not so: they had succeeded in becoming individuals.

As we come to conclusions for this chapter, we find it difficult to assess the relative importance of heredity and the relative importance of environment, which was different for each pattern of twinship. Our subjects led us to conclude that parental interaction was the determinant of psychological separation and individuation in twins. In addition we found that intrapsychic conflict between twins was also a determinant of their psychological separation and individuation.

8

EMPATHY IN TWINS

A DEFINITION
OF EMPATHY
Simply stated, *empathy* is the ability to identify with the feelings of another to the extent that the other understands the presence of the communication. *Webster's Third International Dictionary* (1971) defines *empathy* as:

1. *the imaginative projection of a subjective state whether affective conative or cognitive into an object so that the object appears to be infused with it. . . . The reading of one's own state of mind or conation into an object. . . .*
2. *the capacity for participating in or a vicarious experiencing of another's feelings, volitions, or ideas; and sometimes another's movements to the point of executing bodily movements resembling his. . . . (p. 742)*

Up until this point, our emphasis has been on how twins become psychologically separate from one . another, the intrapsychic process of identity formation in twins. The patterns of twinship described earlier suggest that there are various forms of separation and individuation between twins. Although among the twins we interviewed there were varieties of patterns of separation and individuation, there was a shared feature to these patterns of twinship that was reflected in the problem of separation and individuation. We have defined this commonality as an ability to share with another person and a need for closeness in interpersonal relationships—empathy. "Empathy is honed by the time you can move" was the statement of one competitive identity twin, who gave evidence concerning how early in life this process takes place.

CLOSENESS AND SHARED EXPERIENCES On the basis of these interviews, we concluded that twins share a closeness and a sense of security with each other that would be hard to match in most other relationships. One twin pointed out that for her "twins are born married." Whereas we have stressed the difficulties that twins face in separating, we should qualify the point and indicate that the degree of closeness and security the twinship holds in an affirmative force in the lives of these twins. Thus, while there is certainly a force driving twins to differentiate and individuate, there is also a compelling need to remain close so that they can share their emotional lives and reaffirm their own sense of self. One twin, while reflecting on her relationship with her sister, said, "Between us there is a lot of separateness and a lot of closeness."

Those things that are truly unique about twinship are the degree of closeness and the number of shared experiences that twins have while growing up together. Furthermore, the constant presence of the other is experienced at a time in development when the mother-child bond for all infants is crucial. Twins have an early childhood experience that is different from single children. One twin stated, "The experience of growing up as a twin wouldn't be so hard to understand if everyone was born as a twin."

To understand empirically how twins separate psychologically from one another, and to understand the psychological significance of the continual presence of another, observational studies such as those conducted by Mahler (1967) and her associates would have to be done. However, we feel that we can extrapolate from Mahler's work to understand the significance of the continual presence of another individual during infancy and early childhood.

Describing the psychological birth of the human infant, Mahler suggests that the mother's relationship with her child and the mother's capacity to meet the needs of her child are the critical determinants of well-functioning individuals. The mother who is less capable of fostering psychological growth cannot pick up clues from her child, with the result that the child has a harder time individuating from the mother. How does the presence of the twin sibling affect the early mother-child relationship? Does the presence of the twin matter? Do twins meet each other's needs in a way that the mother cannot understand or replicate?

We do not have definitive answers to these questions. From one twin subject we know, however, that her earliest recollection, the presence of her twin sister's leg close to her own in her crib, is related to her insight that the physical presence of her sister has continued throughout her life to be reassuring to her.

The ways in which a twin sibling affects the mother-child relationship are among the most engaging issues one can raise pertaining to development. What are the effects of the continual presence of another on twin development? The primary relationship between mother and child is influenced in subtle and complicated ways by the compelling presence of a twin. In essence a partial answer to this question emerges from an understanding of the process by which mothers of twins create differences between their twins or respond to differences between their twins.

It is necessary for the mother of twins to make distinctions. However, infant twins cannot distinguish among the mother, the self, and the twin. The givens of the earliest intertwin experiences and the givens of the mother-child experiences are similar. Primitive ego boundaries exist between and among the mother and the twins; the fluidity of ego boundaries between young twins sets the scene for what can be the challenge of individuation and the ability to empathize with others in the future.

How can each twin become "the center of the universe" rather than an incomplete aspect of a whole person? We think that this lack of wholeness—while it creates problems for the process of individuation—also allows for the earliest involvement with a significant other, the twin. This early forerunner of the development of empathy is founded upon the constant physical and psychological presence of the other, with whom one must share the "center of the universe." The sense of security resulting from the presence of the other is established very early in life, and the need for the close presence of another remains throughout the lives of twins. Furthermore, a sense of security or well-being is based upon the nature of the mother-child relationship as well as the relationship with the twin.

THE RE-CREATION OF TWINSHIP   Among the twins we interviewed we found that most had sought to establish close and intense relationships with people. "I have many very close friends," stated a competitive identity twin. They had little tolerance for superficial relationships. "I am concerned with knowing people," stated another twin. These twins found close relationships more meaningful than a series of acquaintanceships. For some of these twins, there were problems with the wish for intense friendships because when they reflected on the need for closeness, it seemed to them a re-creation of their original twinship. They might be disappointed in others because they could not attain the degree of closeness experienced with the twin. Conversely, the friends or partners of such twins had difficulty understanding the requirements of these relationships.

The statement "I have covert expectations that others will understand me" reflected the expectations of many of the twins we talked to. "I cannot understand what you're thinking, you have to tell me" was a common refrain heard early in their marriage by many of our twin subjects. Interestingly enough, most spouses of the twins we interviewed felt that they had special insight into twinship because of their marriages to twins.

Understanding the need to re-create twinship in friendships or marriage was necessary for these twins in order for them to function as successful and comfortable individuals. Resolving this type of conflict took different forms for different individuals. The interdependent twins did not resolve the conflict and continued as best of friends. Some twins clarified their disappointments in relationships through psychotherapy. Experiences with reality were also meaningful in resolving this conflict. For example, a twin reported that the issue of loss of an important relationship was central to resolving a depression that she related to the separation from her twin years earlier.

In fact the need to re-create twinship seemed to be a developmental issue that was more intensely experienced as a problem at the time of initial separation from a twin sibling. The need to re-create twinship loses its significance over time, but it does recur from time to time for most of the twins we interviewed. In other words twins never give up their concerns about the quality of relationships, but they are less concerned about relating authentically in every situation as they grow older. One twin shared with us that he felt that "this is the one time in my life I haven't had a twin friend, another male counterpart. I'm twinning less but I miss it."

LANGUAGE DEVELOPMENT AND EMPATHY Growing up with a twin sibling made our twin subjects more aware and more adept at communication—more empathic. These twins were highly articulate. None of the twin subjects reported having any language difficulties in childhood. This finding contradicts a large body of research that suggests there is a developmental lag in language for young twins (Davis 1937; Day 1932; Koch 1966; Lytton 1980; Malstrom 1980; Mittler 1971).

Moreover, several twins in our study told us about special languages they had developed for fantasy play activities, which were definitely set apart from their verbal communications with the rest of their families or friends. Some of these twins were to some degree able to differentiate among the languages that they used for different purposes at a very young age. A pair of twins reported that as 4- and 5-year-olds they developed a fantasy land that included its own language. They included one or two close friends in this fantasy land, and they used signal words in everyday functioning to clue each other about their feelings and impressions of their reality. Each of these twins had a new twin in their created land.

Another fascinating aspect of communication between twins was the reported ability to communicate nonverbally as children and as adults. Furthermore, twins were aware at a young age that they had an ability to communicate nonverbally. For example, one set of twins described to us that their nonverbal communication was based on sign language and certain body language. This communication was also used to describe feelings about ensuing reality experiences.

Several pairs of twins reported extrasensory perception (ESP) experiences that were concerned with the health and well-being of their twin sibling. For example, one twin stated that she knew something was wrong with her sister and called home to find that her sister had just broken her leg. Another set of twins explained how one of them checked into the hospital for excruciating pain, while her sister was having surgery in another hospital in a faraway city.

A humorous story was related to us by a set of twins who concluded that ESP was at work when, in a tie store overcrowded with literally thousands of ties, each of these twins selected the same tie from opposite sides of the store. Our explanation of these phenomena is based on the shared experiences of these twins and on their ability to communicate with each other nonverbally.

From the interview material we found that the use of language was highly developed in our twin subjects. This finding is attributed to the need of these twins for meaningful communication both verbal and nonverbal and also to their ability to empathize with their twin and with others.

EMPATHY AS A POSITIVE DYNAMIC OF TWINSHIP   The continual presence of a twin sibling creates problems for separation and individuation from the twin as well as from the mother. The process of separation-individuation has been alluded to by psychoanalytic theorists (Burlingham 1952; Engel 1975;

Leonard 1961; Seimon 1980; Tabor and Joseph 1961) and has been described theoretically and empirically in several chapters of this book. Our feeling is that one of the consequences of the continual presence of a twin sibling leads to a positive dynamic, i.e., to the ability to understand and to be able to feel compassionately with and for others.

This ability to be empathic with others, to allow a sense of separateness from another to dissipate, is based on the early twin relationship where ego boundaries are fluid and separateness is not experienced clearly in a psychological sense. Twins learn early in life to identify with the feelings of their sibling, and thus later in life they can identify with the feelings of others while at the same time maintaining closeness with their twin sibling. Twins are also more accustomed to projecting their feelings and thoughts onto others. In this manner, too, they may more quickly engage other people with them. One twin subject said this in her own words: "Twins early in life can identify and project feelings onto each other, and later in life they can identify and project onto others."

The ability to understand how another person is feeling was used positively by our twin subjects. In other words we did not find that our subjects used their ability to cross into the ego boundaries of another as a way of losing their sense of separateness. They did not take on the identity of others or lose themselves under the umbrella of another. Rather, they attempted to understand how others were feeling and then used this knowledge to fulfill their needs for closeness as well as to be supportive of another.

Empathy as a dynamic force in the lives of twins is illustrated by the fact that the majority of the sample were mental health professionals, teachers, or artists. They chose occupations that required an ability to be introspective. For some twins this meant an emphasis on the ability to understand another person in relationship to the self. For the artists among the subjects, being in touch with one's self was given greater emphasis. Some of our subjects stated that they felt their choice of professions was based on their need to be close to others and to help others, whether through an understanding of another's feelings or through artistic self-expression and creativity.

We were told in many different ways about the capacity for closeness between twins and with others. "I have a style of intimacy other people enjoy but can't have," one twin felt. "Even though twinship is the most charged relationship in my life, it has given me a tremendous capacity for intimacy," added another twin. "The capacity to tolerate a lack of ego boundaries and a fascination with being in other people's heads" was the result of another twinship. This subject also felt twinship created "a preoccupation with significant others and a sensitivity to others that single children don't have." He felt that the ability to be empathetic was, on some level, "a searching for his twin again, a denial of separateness." He contended "when twins don't sustain their own separateness, empathy becomes fusion."

The loneliness that twins experience and try to avoid comes from limited experiences alone as infants and children. "Lonliness is oftentimes experienced as a tremendous incompleteness, a fear of the unknown," commented one twin. Along the same line of thought, another twin stated "Merging and being different, alone, is the real issue of twinship." Another twin added that when she needed support or felt lonely, she would call her sister to make her feel less lonely. Clearly, the difficulty that twins experience with loneliness is another aspect of the need for intimacy. The need to be closely associated with another is a consequence of a fear of aloneness and of separateness for twins.

In conclusion, the closeness that twins experience from the time of conception through infancy, childhood, and adolescence is carried over into their adult lives as a need to recreate the twinship, as a need to empathize with others, and as a need for closeness. Twins who resolve the separation from their twin sibling and individuate seek out relationships that are authentic, intense, and psychologically rewarding. Mature twins seek out intimate relationships.

9

THE TWINNING BOND

The twinning bond is a primary relationship originating at the conception of the individual and evolving as a compensatory and/or complimentary relationship along with the development of the mother-child bond. All of the participants were able to describe a primary bond between themselves and their twin.

UNIT IDENTITY   For identical twins with a unit identity, this bond had particular meanings. It is characterized in their earliest memories of "being dressed up and put on stage to perform" or of "attracting attention because there were two of us."

In reflecting on the meaning of the twinning bond, one twin stated, "The bond is a very powerful force in my life. It has influenced us in a way we don't understand but serves to make us never feel totally alone in the world." His twin added that "the bond between us is inevitable, making our lives interrelated. It is larger than us and cannot be overcome."

In another set of identical twins who manifested a unit identity one twin commented, "We started together and we stayed together. Now we have our independence with our husbands and families. Later on we will be back together." Her twin added, "There isn't anything we can't share."

These illustrations indicate the powerful and pervasive quality of the bond between twins with a unit identity. Another dimension of this bond, a predetermined quality of the commitment, is the feeling suggested by one twin who said that she could not see herself without her sister. Indeed, they have always planned to spend their old age together.

INTERDEPENDENT IDENTITY   The bond between twins with an interdependent identity is very intense. One twin with a manifest interdependent bond related, "Our bond is very close. My sister is the first person I think of when I have a problem. This closeness can't be taken away. We feel like a pair. My twin is more important than my mother, who is excluded from the relationship." Her sister said, "The bond is a closeness between us that can't exist with other people."

A fraternal twin stated, "The bond means always having her there, sharing each other's experiences, and a close identification between us." Another identical twin pair saw the bond as a manifestation of sharing everything from the womb on. They added that "we trust each other best."

Twins with interdependent identity have a bond that is unambivalent and all encompassing psychologically. The bond serves to make them highly dependent on one another for emotional support. In that the bond excludes others from the position of most trusted, it serves to limit the importance of other people or other events in their lives. Only things and people who can be shared by this bond are significant to these twins. This bond necessarily excludes the mother.

Interdependent twins' earliest memories involve the close presence of their twin. They agree, "I always remember being a twin and always being together." They cannot imagine not being a twin.

SPLIT IDENTITY   Twins who manifest a split identity do not necessarily see their bond with one another in the same way. The idealized twin usually perceives the bond from a more loving and positive perspective. The devalued twin is usually ambivalent about the relationship.

An identical twin who was devalued in the family felt that she did not have a bond with her sister. But her sister indicated that the bond between them was so strong that nobody could break it. In the same manner, a fraternal twin who had been the victim in the family and consequently spent many years in psychoanalysis stated that she had no need for closeness with her sister. In fact she did not trust her sister, feeling that her twin would use her feelings to her own advantage. She found their fights regressive in that she experienced her sister as wanting to merge with her because "I am the bad part of her." However, her sister seemed to long for closeness and had a very hard time accepting the limits put on the relationship.

After a successful resolution of a split identity, which meant giving up the image of the bad twin through psycho-analysis and self-determination, one identical twin pointed out that the twinning bond no longer existed for her except at times of regression. However her sister, although always ambivalent about the twin relationship, felt the need to defend the closeness of their bond.

Another set of identical twins expressed the ambivalence of split identity in a different way. The idealized twin suggested, "It's [the bond] strange. I am angry that she is not what I want her to be." On the other hand, this twin felt that their bond was intimate and that together they could discover or create new ideas. Her sister, who obviously could not resolve her anger over the rejection from her parents, felt that "the bond is love and being able to talk to someone."

Ambivalence toward the twinship is present in the earliest memories of twins with split identity. One fraternal twin recalled that when she was 7 years old, a neighbor said, "The twins, the twins! Oh, are you one of the twins? What a shame you don't look like your sister. She's so pretty."

IDEALIZED IDENTITY Twins with an idealized identity refer to the "twoness" or team aspects of their relationship. Their earliest memories are of being dressed alike and of acting as a pair. One twin said that their bond meant that "we can share 100% of life's dilemmas and work as a team." His brother added that he felt better together; when his brother was gone, he felt half of himself was missing.

An identical twin who had some degree of separateness stated that the bond meant that her twin would be the first person she would turn to if there was a problem. Her sister said that she would "feel empty without this childhood bond."

Interestingly, another set of twins who idealized their relationship saw the bond between them in different ways. One of them saw the attachment as "greater than any tie including the tie of marriage." While the other twin, who had gained insight into his twinship in psychotherapy, stated that "the bond was a result of a lifelong learning to share experiences. Our bond is not intimate because we have never shared our feelings."

COMPETITIVE TWINS

In describing the bond they feel between themselves, competitive twins note the strength of their feeling for each other. They point out that in caring for each other there is a sense of investment in the other. They also stress that the relationship carries a built-in sense of trust and confidence in each other.

One competitive twin, in defining the twinning bond, stated that for her the attachment of feelings was very deep and multileveled. There was comfort in psychological intimacy as well as in just being together at the same time and the same place. Interestingly, this twin's earliest recollection was of lying close to her twin in a crib. Her twin sister independently recalled as her first twin memory two legs next to each other—the legs of each other.

Another competitive twin described the bond to his brother as "always having a best friend and never feeling alone." He also recalled as the earliest memory of being a twin a physical closeness—being in a twin carriage together.

The quality inherent in twinship of never being alone was viewed with ambivalence by a fraternal twin. This twin felt that the twin bond was a love/hate relationship, and indeed the constant presence of his brother was oppressive. He stated that he had to "turn away from the twin bond to deal with the world."

Another fraternal twin labeled the twin bond as primary, since "twins never have an opportunity to relate to mother separately." The twin relationship was a substitute for the limited attachment to the mother. The twin bond allowed this subject to "gain an identity based on comparison with his brother." This comparison was so encompassing that a great deal of ambivalence was attached to adult experience with his brother. He felt himself slip into a regressed stance whenever comparisons occurred between them.

In general most of the competitive twin subjects felt that their bonds were closer when they were children. These twins were aware that to become individuals they had to decrease the intensity of their closeness, oftentimes requiring that they live geographically far from each other.

Competitive twins, because of the dynamics of their relationship, can excel in comparison with each other and later may discover that as individuals they are also competent and capable. Their ambivalences result from the feelings they still maintain: that their achievements are related to their twinship rather than to their individual efforts. Such a point of view becomes at times threatening to their confidence and provokes regressive feelings. One twin explained the need to separate from her sister to be secure in her own sense of individuality.

Competitive twins were usually separated for the first time in college. They point out how exciting it was to be alone. Indeed, one twin kept her twinship a secret from her classmates because she wanted to be accepted as an individual.

The nature of the twinning bond has determined that these twins will be competitive individuals. They begin again a new series of "races" in their lives and are usually highly successful. The ambivalence felt by these twins does not become a major handicap to them. It seems that the more important aspect of their bond is that they can trust each other and count on one another.

SIBLING
ATTACHMENT
In describing their earliest memories of twinship, fraternal male/female twins usually recall being dressed alike for some special occasion. However, they cannot describe a particular bond between themselves. One twin stated, "We were never into being twins, just brother and sister." His sister added, "The bond is the love between us. I would do anything in my power to help my brother."

"The bond is common experiences and recollections, a sense of empathy and identity that I don't have with my (other) brother," recalled one twin. She also said, "It was fun to get the attention of being a twin. I never felt that I didn't get my full birthday party." Clearly, one aspect that is special about the bond between male/female twins is the feeling of being closer to their twin than to their other siblings.

As this type of bond is only found between twins of different sexes, it appears to be specific to this group. Apparently, male/female twins have less ambivalence about each other than same-sex identical and fraternal twins. This is probably due to the fact that parents and the environment respond to each of them distinctly because they are of different sex.

THE FUNCTIONS
OF THE TWINNING
BOND
These distinctive patterns of twinship bonds evolve from an intricate combination of parental interaction with their twins and the givens of the twin situation (i.e., the continual presence of a twin sibling and, in some cases, genetic similarity) through the process of development. As the reciprocal nature of the mother-child bond is established early in life and varies from one mother and child to another mother and child, so is the twinning bond established at the same time as this primary relationship and varies from twinship to twinship. Therefore, there is no universal or general definition of a *twinning bond*, as has been alluded to in earlier research. The twinning bond is not just ESP, or a special thread between twins, or another romanticized and vague construct. The bond between twins is critical to their development of identity.

Twins can be seen as having two primary forces affecting the development of their identity, the parents and the twin. Our evidence development is unequivocal that identity in twins is affected by twinship. The degree of influence of the twinning bond depends on the nature of mothering twins have experienced.

For those twins who have a unit identity, the bond functions as a singular primary force. As there is almost no mothering, the twins parent each other. They are not able to circumvent the bond.

Twins with an interdependent bond have had limited mothering. They have had to become highly dependent on one another in many aspects of their development. Their bond functions as a compensatory relationship through which these twins will establish their identities.

Those twins who have been divided into good and bad by the mother remain divided. Although they may have been led to believe that they are very close (they are one), by the family and the environment, there is very little closeness or trust between them.

The bond between idealized twins provides them with the identities of being twins and little else. Intimacy and truly deep feelings are not a part of the bond.

Competitively bonded twins have a profound awareness of the depth of their relationship. They are in touch with certain ambivalent feelings that propel them to seek out, in a somewhat overdetermined fashion, their identities.

Male/female twins feel close to each other, but this bond of closeness has less to do with their shared experiences than with their identity formation or their genders.

CONCLUSION   Through empirical descriptions, the nature of the twinning bond has been described as being a function of the relationship created by the parents, both consciously and unconsciously, for their twins. Identity is rooted in this bond, which endures in various manifestations throughout the lives of the twins.

10

IDENTITY AND INTIMACY IN TWINS

Our interest in writing this book was to gain an understanding of the psychological experience of twinship. We felt from our own experiences as twins as well as from our psychological insight and training that growing up as a twin was different from growing up as a single child. Our perception was that nontwins were fascinated by twinship and that the fantasy of having a twin was a common one.

The thoughts and feelings about twinship that nontwins harbored seemed to be stereotypical and one dimensional: twins as copies of one another, twins as opposites of one another. In writing this book we sought not only to dispell the myths and stereotypes about twinship but also to explain to others what it is like to grow up as a twin.

Because we conceived of this study as being innovative and exploratory, we determined that the most helpful twin subjects would be individuals who were motivated to think about their twinships. Furthermore, we believed that successful, well-functioning individuals would be more articulate and insightful about themselves and would, therefore, bear evidence to the differences that exist growing up as twins.

Among these individuals, there were twins who experienced personal problems but who were also able to isolate their problems from their discussions of twinship; therefore, they did not change the nature of a basically well-functioning, successful subject pool.

Our interviews took into account what, for us, were significant theoretical contributions to the child development literature as well as to the relevant research on twin development. The interviews were open-ended but concerned with the following issues: parental reaction to the birth of twins, parental child-rearing practices, emphasis or deemphasis of psychological separateness, separation experiences, language development, friendships outside the twinship, and evolution of the twin relationship.

A REVIEW OF THE FINDINGS OF THE STUDY

Identity formation and the need for authentic relationships with others were predominantly important to the twins who participated in this study. These two central issues grew out of their very roots of identity, the existence of the twinship.

The Mother Creates The Nature of the Twin Relationship

We found that the mother created the nature of the twinning bond through her interactions with her twins, which endured throughout the lives of our twin subjects. The twinning bond or the intertwin relationship patterns are described earlier in the text. Each of these patterns of twinship can be seen as a part of a continuum from psychological closeness to individuation.

Patterns of Twinship

The interview material led us to discern that among our subjects we could distinguish six patterns of twinship. We labeled these patterns unit identity, interdependent identity, split identity, idealized identity, competitive identity, and sibling attachment identity.

The Twinning Bond

The nature of the bond between our twin subjects varied from one pattern of twinship to another. A natural progression of attachment from the very close psychological dependency of unit identity twins to the significant but less intertwined psychological closeness of sibling attachment identity twins evolved from the interview material. There is no single type of attachment between twins.

The Significance of Psychological Separation in Twinship Psychological separation was found to have different meanings for each of the six patterns of twinship. In all cases psychological separation was imperative for individual development. We also found that our twin subjects could tolerate a wide variety of closeness and separateness, depending on the nature of their attachment to one another.

Nature, Nurture, and Interaction The interaction between the mother and child and between the twins was more important than the discernible effects of inheritance or the effects of the broader environment on the establishment of patterns of twinship.

Sex Role Socialization The sibling attachment pattern of twinship supports the importance of early sex role socialization as a determinant of identity formation.

Language Development In opposition to previous research that indicates early language deficits in twin development, none of our subjects reported such experiences. In their current functioning they are articulate and communicative. Indeed, we found that some subjects, as youngsters, developed—in addition to adequate communication skills—a separate communication system that they used discretely, just between themselves. It is our impression that language skills as well as broad communication skills are highly developed in successful, well-functioning adult twins.

Identity Formation in Twins   In addition to the significant role of the mother in the development of identity, twins create differences between themselves as an additional way of establishing a sense of identity.

Conflicts over Psychological Separateness   All of the twin subjects were aware of the conflicts that they had experienced on the path to individuality. Psychological separation from the twin sibling varied among twinship patterns. Perceptions of psychological separateness varied between twins. In this study, e.g., for split identity twins, the good twin felt more attachment to the twin sibling than did the bad twin. The bad twin's attachment to the good twin was destructive to the development of a sense of positive identity.

Empathy in Twinship   Because of the continued presence and awareness of another, twins develop early in life a degree of closeness and a sharing of experiences which leads to empathic relationships with other people.

Competition and Twins   The competitive nature of twin relationships can be used advantageously by twins to develop successful careers and family relationships.

Methodology   Within the parameters of this research, the unstructured, open-ended, but theoretically consistent interview technique produced an abundance of data. The data were clinical in nature. The usefulness of these data was that they did fit with a psychodynamic formulation about child development.

Cultural Stereotypes of Twinship   Cultural stereotypes of twinship are inaccurate and can be detrimental to the development of individuality in twins. For example, not all twins feel very close to each other, yet the stereotype of twinship is that twins should feel close to each other, which can be ultimately confusing and anxiety provoking for twins.

DO MOTHERS CREATE OR RESPOND TO DIFFERENCES IN TWINS? As Erikson (1950), Mahler (1967), and Sullivan (1953) have suggested, we found that the primary mother-child relationship is the cornerstone of twin growth and development. In addition to the mother, twins experience a primary attachment to each other, which has its effect on growth and development. Immediately two questions come to mind: Is the twin relationship as important or more important than the mother-child relationship? Does the mother respond to differences between her twins or does she create them?

On the basis of our interview material, we found that more limited amounts of mothering led to closer bonding between the twins. Conversely, the more adequate the mothering, the better able were the twins to function with the necessary awareness of their twin attachment. The effects of the amount of mothering and the quality of mothering were interrelated with the ability of the mother to respond to or to create differences between her twins.

In the unit identity pattern of twinship, an extreme limitation of mothering meant that there could only be limited responses to the needs of the twin infants, yet these twins developed into well-functioning adults. In this traumatic situation the bond between the twins appears to have served as a compensatory replacement for the mother-child bond.

For interdependent twins in our sample, mothers allowed the twinship to become the primary attachment. These twins frequently stated that they felt they did not need their mothers because they had each other. We believe that such mothers abdicated their roles as primary attachment figures. Why do these mothers allow this pattern of twin-ship to develop? We cannot honestly say why this happens. We can only speculate that perhaps these mothers were so overwhelmed by two children that they had to give the psychological care of the twins to the twins themselves. As the mother did not distinguish between her twins, she did not respond to or create differences between her twins.

Mothers of split identity twins made very clear distinctions between their twins based primarily on projections. From the beginning of life the mother-child relationship was colored by the way in which the mother perceived each child. In addition it may well have been true that certain qualities of the child overdetermined the reactions of the mother. In these instances the mother's response to the twin children may indeed have had some basis in reality (i.e., the twins were temperamentally different), but the overriding factor was the mother's perception of differences between her children. Because in this group of twins the distinctions made were unhealthy and unrealistic, the relationship between the twins was unhealthy and distorted.

From the very beginning of their lives, idealized twins experienced mothering that in all ways supported their twinship and in only a limited fashion supported their thoughts and feelings of individuality. We can speculate that this type of mother perceived differences between her twins quite accurately and responded to these differences. However, differences between twins were secondary to the fact of their twinship. "The twinship" gave these mothers narcissistic gratification.

Mothers of competitive twins were able to respond to the different needs of their children and were therefore able to deal with them as individuals. The bond between these twins was respected by their mothers but was not used as a substitute for the mother-child relationship.

Mothers of sibling identity attachment twins were also able to respond to differences between their twin children. For parents of male/female twins the differences were perhaps most easy to deal with, which led to less emphasis on the attachment between the twins.

We must conclude that the more adequate the mother, the more capable she is of responding to the differences between her twins rather than of creating differences or denying differences. The effect of a single child on a mother is different from the effect of a child who is also a twin. Child rearing for twins becomes a two-way process only when the mother-child relationship is as primary as the twin relationship.

DO TWINS CREATE DIFFERENCES BETWEEN THEMSELVES? Farber (1981) has argued that in their search for individuality twins create artificial differences between themselves. From the interview material we must agree with Farber. In addition the creation of differences as an intrapsychic process between twins was more apparent with less capable mothers. For example, unit identity twins and interdependent identity twins were more compelled to make distinctions between themselves. Twins who had experienced differential treatment by their mothers were less likely to make vivid distinctions between each other.

Burlingham (1952) has suggested that the mother of twins must differentiate between her twins to identify with them and to relate to them. This was not necessarily the case for all twinships. For unit identity twins and for interdependent identity twins, the mother's psychological involvement seemed so minimal that we speculate she did not really make distinctions. In the other patterns of twinship, it appeared that the mother did distinguish between her twins to in order to identify and relate to them.

Differences between twins must be attributed to differences in genetic endowments, the parental interaction, the broader environment, and the interaction between the twins.

IS THERE A RESOLUTION OF THE TWINSHIP? *Twinship* or *twinning* has been defined as either a mutual interdependence between twins or an elusive bond that connects them psychically for as long as they live. Although it would be hard to refute either of these definitions, it appears that twinship is both larger than these parameters for some twins and much less pervasive for other twins. Clearly, there is no one definition of *twinship*. The meaning of *twinship* was personally and existentially defined for each pair of twins with whom we spoke.

In describing patterns of twinship we are attempting to show that there are a variety of twinning bonds and that they are related to the nature of mothering. Within the patterns of twinship there were variations of meanings about the essence of the twin attachment.

There is no way that we can honestly play down the early childhood experience of twinship and the resultant effect on adult identity. Still we must point out that twins dealt with their attachment to one another in different ways—beyond the already described patterns of twinship. The nature of the attachment remained as a unit, interdependent, split into good or bad, idealized, competitive, or similar to a sibling attachment, but the freedom to abandon the attachment or to put it in the past was certainly different for different individuals.

One twin asked us, "Will we ever resolve our relationship?" This question is one that we believe is a concern for all twins. Unit identity twins, on some level, question the integrity of their need for one another. Interdependent twins are aware of their need for one another and seem to have some concern over the close and continual quality of the relationship. Split identity twins have the most conflicts about twinship, but none of them would deny its significance as a determinant of their identity. Idealized identity twins hang onto the notion of twinship but go beyond it to form more intimate and meaningful relationships. Competitive twins see the twinship in adulthood as somewhat of a regression to a stage in their lives where the twin was the focus of their psychic energy, the ideal to strive against. Even though they have put the relationship behind them, they, too, must go back and confront the very closest of attachments to the twin.

Is the relationship with the twin a regression to childhood or adolescence experiences? Is the relationship with the twin a nurturant one, because of the closeness that has been shared for so many years? Certainly the answers to these questions are dependent on the nature of the twinning bond. But in a broader sense we cannot really answer these questions, because having a twin sibling continually present has a long-lasting effect on identity and the formation of other relationships. What does it mean to a twin to turn to his/her twin sibling for comfort? Can the twin trust himself/herself enough to go back to the intensity and intimacy of the twinning bond without losing the separateness other relationships allow? We felt that twins contemplated these questions as adults and looked to themselves for answers because they were so often concerned with maintaining their own identities.

THE NEED FOR CONSTANT REAFFIRMATION OF IDENTITY Not only do twins seem concerned with maintaining their own separate identities, they can also bring a degree of intensity about the very intetrity of their lives to everyday situations, which seems unique to twinship. They are frequently people who question the essence of their beings. They are less likely to be comfortable as followers of trends or ideas, and thus they often persist in following their own paths. Possibly, in these ways such adults are reaffirming their long-sought-after identities.

Being alone is also often a criterion for personal progress that twins note as important. The experience of being alone and independent is very productive and highly desired by twins. In other words, for young adult twins in particular, there is associated with being alone a great sense of achievement or satisfaction from independent accomplishments. The need for continual reaffirmation of identity and for singular accomplishment is an outgrowth of the twinship.

INTIMACY As twins seek out experiences of integrity, they also seek out authentic relationships with other people as well. Their relationships are as important to them as their identity and are rarely superficial. Sometimes twins report that individuals appear to be drawn to them. They are sought after as confidants and trusted friends. These experiences are not accidental since twins themselves are motivated to share themselves with others.

THE ISSUE OF The early attachment to the twin
SEPARATENESS IN creates the need for closeness in other
TWINSHIP relationships. Lichtenstein (1977) has
attempted as a psychoanalyst to understand what he terms
the dilemma of human identity. From his vantage point, he
saw his patients struggling with identity formation in the
following term:

> *They are profoundly torn between an overwhelming yearning to*
> *return to a symbiotic state of existence and an equally com-*
> *pelling urge to assert their separateness as individuals. Their*
> *resolvable conflicts seem due to the fact that both symbiosis and*
> *separateness were equally threatening to the existential*
> *structure of their human reality. Symbiosis implied to them a*
> *ceasing to be, a dissolution of their reality as persons.*
> *Individual separateness, on the other hand, doomed them to*
> *total isolation, as if they were suspended in the void. (p. 9)*

This passage typifies the dilemma of identity for twins.
Separateness and the need for closeness are the turning
points upon which twins must create their own identities.

IMPLICATIONS Although the purpose of the research
FOR was not concerned specifically with
PARENTING appropriate child-rearing strategies,
TWINS the findings and conclusion lead
us to certain recommendations for parenting.

First, we feel that raising twin children is a psychologically demanding experience. The parents of twins need to
have the help and support of others who have had successful
experiences raising twins. As this research indicates the
critical nature of the mother's early encounters with her
children, we suggest that mothers are made aware of the
importance of their interactions with their twin children.

From the findings of this research it became apparent
that making distinctions between twins is critical to their
development as individuals and to their comfort with
twinship and relationships later in their lives.

Mothers need to respond to, rather than to create, differences in their twins. This may be accomplished by tuning into the special needs of each child as much as possible. Twins should be encouraged to make their own choices. Dressing twins alike and giving them the same experiences may be easier for the mother. Twins may come to expect similar treatment from their mothers in many other ways as well; however, this strategy is antithetical to the development of individuality in twins.

Mothers should make as much effort as possible to allow for subtle differences between their twins to develop, whether in the areas of food, clothing, toys, or friendships. Furthermore, mothers should be aware that their twin children will develop very similarly but possibly at slightly different rates. A mother will most likely confront developmental challenges from each twin at slightly different times. For example, one twin may read with greater ease earlier than his twin sibling, who will follow quickly behind and in all likelihood catch up. These minute differences between twins are hardly noticed before circumstances change. Sometimes they even reverse, and mothers must adjust their perceptions of the abilities of their twins in a flexible and often rapid manner.

Those mothers who relate to each child with affection, attention, and flexible perceptual abilities augment growth. Adequate mothers have these abilities. From our interview material it appears that mothers of competitive identity twins were able to provide each twin with affection, attention, and a differentiated perception of individual requirements. The competitive identity twins in our sample were the most successful group personally, as well as professionally.

In addition to adequate mothering, what did the twinship contribute to their success? Twinship can be a supportive relationship. While twins may carefully observe each other's abilities and strive to accomplish what each is capable of, the bond between them permits them to use their knowledge that they are supported and understood by each other as well as by their parents. Successful parenting of twins contributes abundantly to the development of successful individuals.

IMPLICATIONS FOR PSYCHOTHERAPY The implications of twinship as a factor in psychotherapy are solely related to the six patterns of twinship described herein. Thus, they may not apply to all twins seen in psychotherapy. Twins, as do all individuals, have a variety or personal reasons for choosing a course of psychotherapy. Nevertheless, there are some insights that evolve from this research that relate to the process of psychotherapy.

In this study, unit identity twins were able to function well in their careers and in their relationships, but their attachment to one another and the support of each other's ego functioning enabled them to perhaps appear to be better functioning than they would be individually. Psychotherapy with an individual with a unit identity would probably produce as its major challenge the task of stabilizing the ego boundaries of the individual, in addition to dealing with the personal issues the twin brings to the therapy.

Interdependent identity twins are probably least likely to be motivated to involve themselves in psychotherapy because they use each other so willingly in times of stress. An individual interdependent identity twin patient would most likely, immediately, attempt to make the therapy relationship into a twin relationship. These are twins who need to be reminded that they must communicate thoughts and feelings because they cannot be understood by other people without such effort.

Among our group of split identity twins, practically all of the twins had been in some type of psychotherapy. The main dynamic for these individuals to work out was the role that they had been given in the family and had internalized. In therapy these individuals must confront their distorted self-images.

Idealized identity twins would most likely be motivated to understand and to experience a greater range of feelings than their childhood experiences encouraged. These individuals would benefit from a relationship such as the therapeutic relationship, which would give them insight into dealing with other people and support for such efforts.

Competitive identity twins in psychotherapy experience conflict about regressive wishes to reexperience twinship. In addition such individuals are extremely sensitive to and competitive with their therapists. As an outgrowth of their resistance to the regressive aspects of therapy, such individuals will profit enormously from the experience of redefining their twinship. A good many of the twins with competitive identity in this study had been psychoanalyzed.

We did not feel that sibling attachment identity twins are centrally concerned with the fact of their twinship if they choose psychotherapy as a personal experience.

AFTERTHOUGHTS   Upon reflection, we wondered why there were six discrete patterns of twinship found among our sample population. Could there be more patterns of twinship manifested in seemingly psychologically healthy twins? While we have no answer to this question, we have speculated that there may be other variations on the nature of maternal relationships with twins which would conceivably encourage other different patterns of twinship. A more detailed study of mothering twins might yield insights into this issue.

Furthermore, what implications, if any, can be made about other close dyadic relationships from our conclusions about twinship? Clearly, the development of the twinship, an intense sharing experience at the critical stages of development, cannot be replicated. Nevertheless, we feel that aspects of the emotional involvement which twins share may pertain to other intimate relationships. As in well functioning twinships, individuals who have the capacity to empathize with others, and the security of a firm identity maintain relationships that are long enduring and significant.

Does what we have learned about parenting twins have any implications for parenting in general? It would seem that there are such implications. Just as the mother of twins contributes to the individual development of her children, so does the mother of a single child. However, twins grow up differently from single children, because twinship remains at the core of their individual identity.

Appendix

INTERVIEW The following interview was completed with all of the participants. Participants were asked not to discuss the interview material or format with their twin. Both researchers were present at the time of the interview. The order of the questions varied form interview to interview.

1. What is your earliest memory of being a twin?

2. Describe your parents' feelings about having twins (Include economic situation, other siblings in the family).

3. School situation - Were you in the same classes or in separate classes in elementary school as well as in high school? What about college?

4. Did you dress alike? When did you stop dressing alike?

5. Friendships - Who were your friends? Did your twin have the same friends or different friends and when were they the same or different? How about present friendships, what are they like?

6. Did you ever feel you had a unit identity? (We explained this concept)

7. When were you first separated from your twin? What were your feelings about that separation?

8. Did you ever feel you recreated the twinship in other situations or with other people?

9. What do you see as the positive aspects of being a twin?

10. For you, what were the drawbacks of being a twin?

11. Can you describe a special attachment between you and your twin?

12. How would you describe your present relationship with your twin?

BIBLIOGRAPHY

Ainsworth, M. 1974. "Infant Mother Attachment and Social Development." In *The Integration of the Child into a Social World*, edited by M. Richars. London: Cambridge University Press.

Allen, M., S. Greenspan, and W. Pollin. 1976. "The Effect of Parental Perception on Early Development in Twins." *Psychiatry* 39: 65-71.

Bell, R. 1977. *Child Effects on Adults*. New Jersey: Halstad Press.

Bernstein, A., and G. Warner. 1981. *An Introduction to Contemporary Psychoanalysis*. New York: Jason Aronson.

Black, K., and K. Campbell. 1974. "Differential Mental Development of 18 Month Same Sexed and Opposite Sexed Twins." *ERIC Document ED* 101834.

Bower, T. G. R. 1976. *A Primer of Infant Development*. San Francisco: W. H. Freeman Press.

Bowlby, J. 1958. "The Nature of the Child's Tie to His Mother." *International Journal of Psychoanalysis* 39:350-73.

Brody, E., and N. Brody. 1976 *Intelligence: Nature, Determinants and Consequences*. New York: Academic Press.

Burlingham, D. 1952. *Twins: A Study of Three Pairs of Identical Twins*. New York: International Universities Press.

Burlingham, D. 1963. "A Study of Identical Twins." In *The Psychoanalytic Study of the Child* (Vol. 18), edited by R. Eissler. New Haven: Yale University Press.

Chess, S., and A. Thomas. 1963. *Behavioral Individuality in Early Childhood*. New York: New York University Press.

Claridge, G. S., W. Hume, and S. Canter. 1973. *Personality Differences and Biological Variations: A Study of Twins*. New York: Pergamon Press.

Cohen, D., M. Allen, M. Pollin, M. Werner, and E. Dibble. 1972. "Personality Development in Twins." *Journal of the American Academy of Child Psychiatry* 11:625-44.

Cohen, D., E. Dibble, and J. Grave. 1977. "Parental Style in Twin Interaction." *Archives of General Psychiatry* 34:445-51.

Cowan, P. 1978. *Piaget with Feelings*. New York: Holt, Rhinehart and Winston.

Davis, E. A. 1937. *The Development of Linguistic Skill in Twins, Singletons, and Sibs, and Only Children from 5-10.* Institute of Child Welfare, University of Minnesota, Minneapolis.

Day, E. 1932. "The Development of Language in Twins: A Comparison of Twin and Single Children." *Child Development* 3:298-316.

Dibble, E., and D. Cohen. 1981. "Personality Development in Identical Twins: The First Decade of Life." *Psychoanalytic Study of the Child* 36:45-70.

Dworkin, R. 1979. "Genetic and Environmental Influences on Person Situation Interactions." *Journal of Personality* 13:279-93.

Elkind, D. 1970. *Children and Adolescents: Essays on Jean Piaget.* New York: Oxford University Press.

Engel, G. L. 1975. "The Death of a Twin: Mourning and Anniversary Reactions: Fragments of 10 Years of Self-Analysis." *International Journal of Psychoanalysis* 45:23-40.

Erikson, E. 1950. *Childhood and Society.* New York: W. W. Norton.

Erikson, E. 1968. *Identity: Youth and Crisis.* New York: W. W. Norton.

Eysenck, H. J. 1967. *The Biological Basis of Personality.* Springfield, Ill.: Charles C. Thomas.

Farber, S. 1981. *Twins Reared Apart: A Reanalysis.* New York: Basic Books.

Flavell, J. H. 1963. *The Developmental Psychology of Jean Piaget.* Princeton, N.J.: Van Nostrand.

Floderus-Myrhed, B., N. Pederson, and I. Rasmuson. 1980. "Assessment of Heritability for Personality Based on a Short Form of the Eysenck Personality Inventory, a Study of 12,898 Twin Pairs." *Behavioral Genetics* 10:153-61.

Foch, T., M. O'Connor, R. Plomin, and T. Sherry. 1980. "A Twin Study of Specific Behavioral Problems of Socialization as Viewed by Parents." *Journal of Abnormal Child Psychology* 81:189-99.

Gessell, A. 1941. "Comparative Studies of Twin T. and C." In *Genetic Psychological Monographs*, edited by C. Murchison. Provincetown, Mass.: Journal Press.

Gessell, A., and H. Thompson. 1941. "Twins T. and C.: From Infancy to Adolescence." In *Genetic Psychological Monographs*, edited by C. Murchison. Provincetown, Mass.: Journal Press.

Gifford, S., B. Muraski, T. Berry Brazelton, and G. Young. 1966. "Differences in Individual Development within a Pair of Identical Twins." *International Journal of Psychoanalysis* 47:261-68.

Goldsmith, H., and I. Gottesman. 1981. "Origins of Variation in Behavioral Style: A Longitudinal Study of Temperament in Young Twins." *Child Development* 52:91-103.

Gromada, K. 1981. Maternal - Infant Attachment: The First Step Toward Individualizing Twins. *Maternal Care Nursing Journal* 6:129-34.

Harper, R. 1959. *Psychoanalysis and Psychotherapy 36 Systems.* Princeton, N.J.: Prentice-Hall.

Hift, K. 1980. "An Experimental Study of the Twinning Reaction and Ego Development." Ph.D. dissertation, Adelphi University.

Hinsie, L., and R. Campbell. 1970. *Psychiatric Dictionary* (4th ed.). New York: Oxford University Press.

Ho, H., T. Foch, and R. Plomin. 1980. "Developmental Stability of the Relative Influence of Genes and Environment on Specific Cognitive Abilities during Childhood." *Developmental Psychology* 16:340-46.

Holden, C. 1980. "Twins Reunited." *Science* 215:54-60.

James, Henry (editor). 1920. *The Letters of William James*, Vol. 1, Boston: The Atlantic Monthly Press.

Jensen, A. R. 1969. "Hierarchical Theories of Mental Ability." In *On Intelligence*, edited by B. Dockrell. London: Mitchum.

Kaplan, L. 1978. *Oneness and Separateness: From Infant to Individual.* New York: Simon and Schuster.

Koch, H. 1966. *Twin and Twin Relations.* Chicago: University of Chicago Press.

Leonard, M. 1961. "Problems in Identification and Ego Development in Twins." In *The Psychoanalytic Study of the Child* (Vol. 16), edited by R. Eissler. London: Hogarth Press.

Lichtenstein, H. 1977. *The Dilemma of Human Identity.* New York: Jason Aronson.

Luria, A. R. and F. Yudovitch. 1959. *Speech and the Development of Mental Process in the Child.* London: Staple Press.

Lytton, H., D. Conway, and R. Suave. 1977. "The Impact of Twinship on Parent-Child Interaction." *Journal of Personality and Social Psychology* 35:97-107.

Lytton, H., N. Martin, and L. Evaes. 1977. "Environmental and Genetical Causes of Variation in Ethological Aspects of Behavior in 2 Year Old Boys." *Social Biology* 24:200-11.

Lytton, M. 1980. *Parent Child Interaction.* New York: Plenum Press.

Mahler, M. 1967. *The Psychological Birth of the Human Infant.* New York: Basic Books.

Malstrom, P. 1980. "Manifestation of Twinship in Toddler Language." *Proceedings of the 6th Annual Berkeley Linguistic Society* 16:361-68.

Matheny, A. 1980. "Bayley's Infant Behavior Record: Behavioral Components and Twin Analysis." *Child Development* 51:1157-67.

Matheny, A., and A. Dolan. 1980. "A Twin Study of Personality and Temperament during Middle Childhood." *Journal of Research and Personality.* 14:224–34.

Matheny, A., A. Dolan, and R. Wilson. 1976. "Twins: Within-Pairs Similarity on Bayley's Infant Behavior Record." *Journal of Genetic Psychology.* 128: 263–70.

Mittler, P. 1971. *The Study of Twins.* London: Penguin Books, Inc.

Munsinger, H., and A. Douglas. 1976. "The Syntactic Abilities of Identical and Fraternal Twins and Their Siblings." *Child Development* 47:40-50.

Muss, E. 1982. "Social Cognition: David Elkind's Theory of Adolescences." *Adolescence* 17:33-45.

Newman, H., F. N. Freeman, and K. J. Holzinger. 1937. *Twins: A Study of Heredity and Environment.* Chicago: University of Chicago Press.

Niels Juel-Nielsen, J. N. 1980. *Individual and Environment: Monozygotic Twins Reared Apart.* New York: International University Press.

Osborne, R., and D. Suddick. 1973. "Stability of I.Q. Differences in Twins Between Ages of Twelve and Twenty." *Psychological Reports* 32:1096-98.

Paluszny, M., and B. Beht-Hallahni. 1974. "An Assessment of Monozygotic Twin Relationship by the Semantic Differential." *Archives of General Psychiatry* 31:110-17.

Paluszny, M., and R. Gibson. 1974. "Twin Interactions in a Normal Nursery School." *American Journal of Psychiatry* 13:293-96.

Piaget, J. 1932. *The Moral Judgment of the Child.* London: Kegan Paul.

Piaget, J. 1950. *The Psychology of Intelligence.* London: Routledge.

Piaget, J. and B. Inhelder. 1969. *The Psychology of The Child.* New York: Basic Books.

Plomin, R., and D. Rowe. 1977. "A Twin Study of Temperament in Young Children." *Journal of Psychology* 97:107-13.

Plomin, R., and K. Willerman. 1975. "A Cotwin Control Study of Reflection-Impulsivity in Children." *Journal of Educational Psychology* 47:537-43.

Rowe, D. 1981. "Environmental and Genetic Influences on Dimensions of Perceived Parenting: A Twin Study." *Developmental Psychology* 17:203-8.

Rowe, D., and R. Plomin. 1979. "Environmental Influences in Infants Social Responsiveness." *Behavioral Genetics* 9:519-25.

Scarr-Salaptik, S. 1973. "Race, Social Class and I.Q." *Science* 182:1042-47.

Scarr-Salaptik, S., and L. Carter-Saltzman. 1979. "Twin Method: Defense of a Critical Assumption." *Behavioral Genetics* 9:527-42.

Schave, B. 1982. "Similarities and Differences in 6-Year Old Identical and Fraternal Twins and Their Parents on Measures of Locus of Control and Normal Development." Ed.D. dissertation, University of Southern California.

Scheinfield, A. 1967. *Twins and Supertwins.* New York: Lippincott.

Seimon, M. 1980. "The Separation-Individuation Process in Adult Twins." *American Journal of Psychotherapy* 35:387-400.

Shields, J. 1962. *Monozygotic Twins Brought Up Apart and Together.* London: Oxford University Press.

Smith, N. 1976. "Longitudinal Personality Comparison in One Pair of Identical Twins." *Catalog of Selected Documents in Psychology* 6:106.

Sullivan, H. 1953. *The Interpersonal Theory of Harry Stack Sullivan.* New York: W. W. Norton.

Tabor, J., and E. Joseph. 1961. "The Simultaneous Analysis of a Pair of Identical Twins and the Twinning Reaction." In *The Psychoanalytic Study of the Child* (Vol. 16), edited by R. Eissler. New Haven: Yale University Press.

Thorndike, E. 1905. *Measurement of Twins.* New York: Science Press.

Torgensen, M., and E. Kringlen. 1978. "Genetic Aspects of Temperamental Differences in Infants." *Journal of the American Academy of Child Psychiatry* 17:433-44.

Vandenberg, S., and K. Wilson. 1979. "Failure of the Twin Situation to Influence Twin Differences in Cognition." *Behavioral Genetics* 9:58-60.

Warner, W. L. 1960. *Social Class in America*. New York: Harper Brothers.

Webster's Third New International Dictionary. 1971. Springfield Mass.: G & C Merriam Company Publishers.

Werner, E. 1973. "From Birth to Latency: Behavioral Differences in a Multi-Racial Group of Twins." *Child Development* 44:438-44.

Wilson, R. 1975. "Twins: Patterns of Cognitive Development as Measured on the Wechsler Pre-School and Primary Scale of Intelligence." *Developmental Psychology* 11:126-34.

Wilson, R. 1978. "Synchronies in Mental Development: An Epigenetic Perspective." *Science* 202:939-47.

Wilson, R., A. Brown, and A. Matheny. 1971. "Emergence and Persistence of Behavioral Differences in Twins." *Child Development* 42:1381-98.

Wilson, R., and E. Harring. 1977. "Twins and Siblings: Concordance for School-Age Mental Development." *Child Development* 48:211-16.

Zazzo, R. 1960. *Les Jumeaux, le couple et la personne*. Paris: Presses Universitaires de France.

ABOUT THE AUTHORS

BARBARA SCHAVE is the coordinator of the parent/infant toddler program at USC School for Early Childhood Education, where she has worked for the last four years with undergraduates, teachers, parents and children. She has published articles on dance for children, personality development in young twins, and has co-authored a book on curriculum development. Dr. Schave holds a A.B. from the University of California, Berkeley, an M.S. from the University of Southern California, and an Ed.D. from the University of Southern California in child development. Dr. Schave is an identical twin.

JANET CIRIELLO is a clinical psychologist in private practice in Beverly Hills. She also serves on the staff of the Reiss-Davis Child Study Center in Los Angeles. Dr. Ciriello received her A.B. from Sarah Lawrence College, an M.S. in experimental psychology from the University of Pittsburgh and an Ed.D. from the Harvard Graduate School of Education. Dr. Ciriello received a Fulbright Fellowship for psychological studies in France. Dr. Ciriello is an identical twin.